STUDY GUIDE
by Sherry Harney

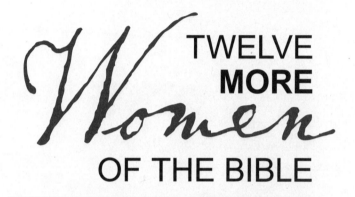

TWELVE
MORE
Women
OF THE BIBLE

LIFE-CHANGING STORIES
FOR WOMEN TODAY

12 SESSIONS

Based on teaching from:

KAREN EHMAN, BIANCA JUÁREZ OLTHOFF,
LISA HARPER, CHRYSTAL EVANS HURST,
MARGARET FEINBERG, COURTNEY JOSEPH

Harper*Christian*
Resources

CONTENTS

INTRODUCTION

Transparent Portraits

Beautifully honest! That is what the Bible is.

From the creation of the first man and woman in the opening chapters of Genesis to the glorious consummation of all things in the closing pages of Revelation, the Bible paints pictures of people as they really were—with all their human struggles, doubts, and failings. This includes the portrayals of women who followed God and lived by faith.

The women you meet in the Bible, including those you will learn about in this twelve-session study, will impress, surprise, and inspire you. The sessions in this study are intended to help you see these women as they lived and to see yourself as you can be through an ever-growing faith in Jesus. Their lives were not perfect—and your life will not be perfect either. But their lessons and journeys of faith are recorded in the pages of God's Word to help you find your way forward as you follow God's leading in every possible situation.

Some of these women show up in a single paragraph of the Bible and then disappear back into history. You have only a glimpse of their story, but it still speaks volumes. You can learn much from these often missed and passed over women of faith.

Other women have entire books of the Bible written about them. You get to follow them through years of their life. These women give you a fully orbed vision of a real person, walking with God, seeking after their Maker. Their stories give you hope that every year of your life can offer time to grow in faith and walk more closely with God.

In every account, you meet women filled with the presence and power of the living God. Their appearance in the Bible, be it brief or expansive, is divinely ordained. Their lessons are eternal. Their lives matter to God, and they should matter to each of us as well.

May God anoint your study of these unique and beautiful women, deepen your faith, and grow your passion to follow Jesus.

PROVERBS 31 WOMAN

HOW NOT TO DO IT ALL

Key Scripture: Proverbs 31:10–31

Karen Ehman

MEETING THE PROVERBS 31 WOMAN

*T*his woman is unreal! Literally. All of the other women you will meet in this twelve-session study are captured in a real place and time. Each of their stories comes from a particular context and setting in biblical history.

But not the woman portrayed in Proverbs 31. While she may be based on an actual person, the collection of her qualities and attributes are gathered from a lifetime of experiences and lessons learned. This chapter in Proverbs is not grounded on one moment in time. The portrait painted is a highlight reel, a "best of" collection, a top ten list.

The Proverbs 31 Woman is an ideal meant to inspire you to noble living, passionate leadership, humble service, compassionate care, and authentic faith. She is not meant to discourage you by setting the bar too high. Instead, she is a picture of beauty, grace, kindness, industry, and passion for life, meant to give you hope and inspiration.

As you read about this woman of noble character, listen for the whisper of the Holy Spirit. God inspired these words to give you something to strive toward—a vision of who you can be. God loves you as you are, but he also calls you to keep growing into the woman you long to be. Let the Proverbs 31 Woman be your example.

Introduction

Picture perfect! It is an old saying that continues to cut at our heart and soul. When we view another person and see a snapshot frozen in time, we actually believe the image in front of us tells the whole story. It might be a Christmas picture of a family where everyone is smiling, well dressed, and apparently quite in love with each other. Everyone is delighted to be there, and peace is etched on every face. That is what the picture seems to convey.

Snap! There it is . . . a perfect family, couple, or life.

In recent years, this picture-perfect life has been expanded from one yearly snapshot to weekly or daily posts on social media. These images become a highlight reel of only the best experiences, the most exciting adventures, the most precious moments, and the happiest happenings. When we see these images, we might forget that any life can look glorious if we push the button at exactly the right moment, delete the pictures that did not turn out well, post only the highlights, and bury the mess and pain that surround these digital moments frozen in time.

At first glance, a couple named Carlos and Maria appeared to have such a picture-perfect life. They had a nice home, new cars, and smiles from ear to ear. A couple of times a year, they would host a party at their home and invite friends, neighbors, and church leaders over. It was a guaranteed afternoon of food, games, and laughter. No one knew that when the party was over, the house grew very silent. Maria and Carlos would both retreat to neutral ground and do their best to get along.

Suzette also seemed to have a picture-perfect existence. She loved life, people, and Jesus most of all. She had lots of friends and possessed a heart to serve those in need. Her voice was beautiful, and everyone at church felt drawn into the presence of Jesus when they heard her sing on the worship team. Her joy was real and deep, but so was her loneliness and depression. She let the joy shine for others to see, but she kept the dark days to herself.

Picture-perfect lives, marriages, and families exist only in fantasy. Real lives are a ruggedly beautiful mosaic made of laughter and tears, victory and defeat, confidence and worry, songs and laments, and a host of other highs and lows. This is true in our lives today and equally true of the people who lived in the days the Bible was inspired by the Holy Spirit of God.

Talk About It

Briefly respond as a group to one of the following questions.

Tell a fun story about a picture time with your family that was particularly challenging. How did the picture finally turn out (or not turn out)?

Tell about a character in the Bible you really appreciate. How is his or her story a combination of both wonderful strengths and honest human struggle?

All of us could have a unique poem written about us.

—Karen Ehman

Video Teaching Notes

As you watch the teaching segment for session one, use the following outline to record anything that stands out to you.

Social media and the challenge of presenting a life in picture-perfect moments

Is the woman described in Proverbs 31 meant to be envied, emulated . . . or something else?

Our reactions to this woman: usually one of two things

Who is this woman . . . she is more than meets the eye

What can we learn from this woman?

1. It's about what you do and how you do it

2. Identify what is unique

3. Don't let comparison boss you around

4. Know your true audience

5. Have healthy fear

6. Remember the ruby

It is always best to be an original version of yourself than a cheap, knockoff imitation of somebody else.

—Karen Ehman

Small Group Study and Video Discussion

Take a few minutes with your group members to discuss what you just watched and explore these concepts in Scripture.

1. What are some of the dangers of fixating on social media (or similar picture-perfect depictions) and believing these are real and honest presentations of other people's lives? Have you ever found yourself envious of such seemingly problem-free individuals?

2. **Read** Proverbs 31:10–31. What are some of the positive and praiseworthy characteristics you see in the woman portrayed in this passage? Why is it valuable and helpful to think about these traits and even aspire to grow them in our lives?

3. The list of qualities and characteristics of this woman is most likely a composite of a lifetime of good moments and not the whole story of her experiences. (The times of struggle, sin, and hardship are not featured in this short list.) When we realize this is more of a highlight reel rather than an inclusive feature length film, we can open our hearts to learn from this woman's accomplishments. Imagine that someone wrote a list of your best moments and character traits that come from your faith in Jesus and love for God. What are at least three positive and God-pleasing things they would write about you?

-
-
-

Share one of these statements with your group members and humbly celebrate this good and beautiful work of God in your life. Be sure to share how this trait or characteristic has grown and developed over the years as you have walked with Jesus.

4. If the woman in Proverbs 31 is actually a picture of Bathsheba, the wife of David and mother of Solomon, how would this reality round out the fact that she was a real person with beautiful strengths and painful flaws? How does seeing the whole person—and not just the picture-perfect image—actually help us learn from a person's life?

5. Take time as a group to "translate" some of this woman's activities and traits. What might this look like in our world today?

Verse	Then:	Now:
13	She selects wool and flax and works with eager hands.	
16	She considers a field and buys it; out of her earnings she plants a vineyard.	
20	She opens her arms to the poor and extends her hands to the needy.	
21	When it snows, she has no fear for her household; for all of them are clothed in scarlet.	
27	She watches over the affairs of her household and does not eat the bread of idleness.	
28	Her children arise and call her blessed; her husband also, and he praises her.	

What is one of these traits you long to develop and deepen in your life? How can your group members pray for you and encourage you as you seek to grow this characteristic?

Do what you can; don't do what you can't.

—*Karen Ehman*

6. This list of characteristics in Proverbs 31 is not a "to do" list of stuff we must accomplish immediately but a "ta da!" list of things God wants to grow in us over time for his glory. What is one "ta da!" moment you have seen in your own life in the past month? How did your awareness of spiritual growth bring joy and delight when you saw how God was working in and through your life?

7. God cares not just about *what* we do in life but also about *how* we do it. What do you notice in this regard about the attitude and disposition of the woman in Proverbs 31? What can we learn from her example?

8. Why is playing the comparison game dangerous and deadly when it comes to our health and joy? What are ways we can focus more on who God is making us and our family? How can we fight against the temptation to compare ourselves to other women and our family to other families?

> *Stop comparing. Throw confetti instead, commending each woman and her uniqueness.*
>
> —*Karen Ehman*

9. **Read** Colossians 3:23–24. What are some possible consequences and problems we might face if we expect our family members to praise us and vocally appreciate all we do? How can living with God as our primary and only true audience bring greater joy and confidence as we love and serve others?

How can a deep reverence and awe of God inspire us to live fully for Jesus?

10. Each one of us is God's ruby . . . unique, rare, and beautiful. What is one thing you can share about each person in your group that you see as rare, striking, and honoring to God?

I need to remember I am loving and serving for an audience of One.

—*Karen Ehman*

Closing Prayer

Spend time in your group praying in any of the following directions:

- Thank God that you do not need to live a picture-perfect life because Jesus gave himself as the perfect Savior and lover of your soul.

- Thank God that the Bible is filled with portrayals of people with powerful strengths and honest brokenness.

- Pray for freedom from playing the comparison game. Ask God to help you focus on becoming the woman he wants you to be and not a replica of some other woman.

- Invite the Holy Spirit to shape your attitudes and motivations so that you will learn to do the right things in the right ways for God's glory.

- Ask God to grow in you a holy and powerful awe and reverence for his glory, power, and love.

No one can do it all, all at once.

—*Karen Ehman*

Reflect on the material you have covered during this session by engaging in any or all of the following between-sessions activities. Remember this is not about following rules or doing your homework—these activities are designed to help you apply the concepts in a practical way during the week. Be sure to make a note of any questions or comments that arise from the activities that you would like to discuss at your next group meeting.

An Aspirational Acrostic

In the video, Karen explained that the passage of the Bible covered in this session is actually an acrostic. This was a poetic structure used in the ancient world in which each line began with a letter of the Hebrew alphabet in order from first to last.

Today, take time to make your own acrostic of characteristics you see in yourself, or want to see grow in the years to come. Come up with one word or a short sentence for each letter of the alphabet. For instance, you might say: "A—*admiring* others; B—notice *beauty* around me; C—show *compassion* consistently" . . . you get the idea.

Have some fun with this, and remember it is not meant to be a "to do" list that causes pressure or guilt. It should be a "ta da!" list that inspires you and leads you to praise when you see yourself taking steps forward in any of the areas you list. Be sure to include some strengths you have already so you can "ta da!" as you write your list.

Characteristics, Attitudes, and Aspirations:

A —

B —

C —

D —

E —

F —
G —
H —
I —
J —
K —
L —
M —
N —
O —
P —
Q —
R —
S —
T —
U —
V —
W —
X —
Y —
Z —

"Ta Da!" to You

Take time in the coming week to send a few texts, emails, or handwritten notes to three women in your life who have been an example of godly character. Let each one know that God has used her to show you how a woman of God can love, serve, worship, lead, and impact the world. Thank her for seeking Jesus, and let her know that you are stronger in faith and striving to live more for God's glory because of her life.

1. Name: _____

   Characteristics and God-honoring traits I see in this woman:

   ●

   ●

   ●

2. Name: _____

   Characteristics and God-honoring traits I see in this woman:

   ●

   ●

   ●

3. Name: _____

   Characteristics and God-honoring traits I see in this woman:

   ●

   ●

   ●

Ruby Reflections

This might be a difficult and challenging exercise for some women, but it is one that we should all do on occasion. During the teaching session, Karen talked about the unique and beautiful nature of rubies. You are like a ruby because you are made by God (see Psalm 139), and no other woman on planet Earth is exactly like you.

All too often you may look at your uniqueness as a liability or something to be hidden. But God celebrates it! So take time to look at some of the facets of who you are and who you are becoming in Christ. Write down some of the things that make you unique in God's sight. Then thank him for how he has made you—fearfully and wonderfully unique.

Unique aspects of my *spiritual life* and love for Jesus:

●

●

Unique aspects of my *gifting and abilities* as I live for Jesus:

●

●

Unique aspects of my *physical makeup* and how God has made me:

●

●

Unique aspects of my *emotions and passion* and how I love Jesus and others:

●

●

Other unique aspects of who I am in Jesus:

-
-

Once you have made your list, read through it and praise God for the way he has shaped you, and how he is working in you to make you more like Jesus.

Journal

Use the space provided below to write some reflections on any of the following topics:

- Write down aspects of the Proverbs 31 Woman that you see growing in you. How can you delight in these?

- Write about aspects of your character that you sense God wants to grow to make you more the woman he would have you become. What steps can you take to keep growing in this area?

- Write down what gets in the way of you seeing the good things God is doing through you and growing in you. How can you get past these obstacles so you can have more "ta da!" moments of rejoicing in the good things God is doing?

- Write about who needs to hear the lessons you have learned in this study. How can you share these encouraging truths with this person?

DEBORAH

FIGHT LIKE A GIRL

Key Scripture: Judges 4

Bianca Juárez Olthoff

MEETING DEBORAH

*I*n a world dominated by men, Deborah stands out as a beautiful example of strength, leadership, collaboration, and humility. The judges during this time in Israel's history were political and military leaders whom God called to lead his people for a season of revival and revolution. Each judge led the people of God as they fought against their oppressors and turned their hearts back to Yahweh, their Maker and Savior.

Deborah was called to lead during a time that seemed hopeless for God's people. The Israelites were being crushed under the military heel of Jabin, the king of Canaan. His commander, Sisera, had a military machine that was unrivaled at that time and place. For two decades, Jabin and Sisera dominated their part of the world, and the people of Israel were an occupied and oppressed people.

Into this environment God called a new judge, a fresh face of leadership. Deborah was a married woman as well as a prophet of God. She was gifted with wisdom to guide people, situations, and the nation of Israel. In addition to all this, God called her to take military leadership and fight back against the overwhelming and occupying Canaanite forces.

Deborah called a man named Barak to come alongside her in battle. She understood the power of partnership and not doing everything on her own . . . as all the best leaders understand. Deborah not only partnered with Barak in leading the troops into battle but also collaborated with him on writing a victory song of celebration (see Judges 5).

Deborah's life, leadership, and legacy should inspire all of us. She loved and followed God. She heard the call to lead and followed. When God brought victory and deliverance to his people, she was quick to give him the praise and glory.

May God raise up more and more leaders like Deborah.

Introduction

The church is filled with women who are leading in ways that surprise even them! Consider these three stories.

Ann dealt with fear and anxiety for much of her life. As a young girl, she faced deep loss and emotional turmoil when her little sister was killed in a tragic accident. As a mother of six with a passion for family, she was happy staying out of the limelight. *But God had other plans.* Ann took a journey of counting her blessings and ended up writing a book called *One Thousand Gifts.* Now, in addition to being a mom, wife, and follower of Jesus, Ann Voskamp speaks to women around the world, blogs, and stands in the gap for children in poverty as she partners with Compassion International. God has called her to lead in surprising ways, and she has followed faithfully.

Bianca could not read until she was eleven years old. She grew up in a setting that was dangerous, challenging, and sometimes discouraging. Nothing in her childhood would have pointed to her becoming an influential leader. *But God turned her life upside down.* The Holy Spirit captured her heart and called her to action. Now, Bianca Juárez Olthoff not only invests in her two wonderful stepchildren and her marriage but also travels the world as the chief storyteller for the A21 Campaign. She is a powerful voice in the anti–human trafficking movement globally and an author and blogger.

Sherry grew up in a quiet town in West Michigan. She loved Jesus from her childhood and dreamed of being a schoolteacher, wife, and mother. *But God surprised her with additional callings.* After teaching second grade for three years, she felt a call to go to seminary and pursue a degree in theology. Today she is a wife, mother, and teacher as well as the cofounder of Organic Outreach International, a ministry that trains church and movement leaders to mobilize the church outward with the gospel of Jesus. She is also a writer who partners with authors like Ann and Bianca, writing studies like the one you hold in your hand.

If you were to ask any of these women if they saw this coming, they would humbly chuckle and say, "No way!" But each one was willing to follow God's surprising call.

Talk About It

Briefly respond as a group to one of the following questions.

Tell about a time God called you to do something you did not see coming. How did you respond to this surprising call? What has God done through your willingness to follow?

Tell about a time you sensed God calling you to follow him on an adventure, and you resisted or said no because you were afraid. What might God have done if you had followed him? Is there any way you could still take action and follow this call of God?

God is bigger than your history and more concerned with your destiny.

—Bianca Juárez Olthoff

Video Teaching Notes

As you watch the teaching segment for session two, use the following outline to record anything that stands out to you.

Meeting Deborah, a gifted and passionate leader

People are looking for leaders

We all face times when we need help

Meeting Barak, a reluctant leader (and others like him)

● Gideon

● Moses

• Jeremiah

Lessons from Deborah:

1. Leaders speak grace and truth

2. Leaders trust in something bigger than themselves

3. Leaders look different

4. Leaders must be willing

We need to stop seeing the things we are NOT and start believing in a God who IS.

—Bianca Juárez Olthoff

Small Group Study and Video Discussion

Take a few minutes with your group members to discuss what you just watched and explore these concepts in Scripture.

1. Sometimes, we remove ourselves from being a leader by saying things like, "I'm just a mom," or "I'm just a student," or "I'm just a manager." Instead, we should declare with confidence, "I am a child of God!" Why is it dangerous and damaging to play the "I'm just a . . ." game? How might your life change if you confidently believed and proclaimed, "I am a child of God"?

2. **Read** Judges 4:1–5. What was unique about Deborah that made her stand out as a woman in her day? How does this inspire you to be available for God to work in and through you in ways you might not have dreamed or imagined?

   What practical ways does Deborah's example offer to Christian women to take steps forward in leadership right where God has put them?

3. God is more concerned about our destiny than our history. If we stay fixated on problems of the past, how will this become a roadblock to God using us in the future?

   What are some practical ways you have learned to let go of things in your past so you can seek to follow God's call for your future?

> *What you are born into doesn't determine what is IN YOU.*
>
> —*Bianca Juárez Olthoff*

4. **Read** Judges 4:3. The people of Israel were feeling oppressed, depressed, and under the heel of their enemies. After twenty years, they finally cried to the Lord for help—and that is when God sent Deborah. What are some of the ways we can be oppressed and depressed? How can we cry out to the Lord for help?

   What do you need to cry out to God about today? How can your group members cry out to God on your behalf?

5. **Read** Judges 4:6–10. How have you seen God use men and women to serve him together in leadership? How does leadership become more effective and God honoring when both men and women bring their gifts to the leadership table?

6. How does Deborah speak the truth in a gracious and loving way to Barak? Why are we often afraid to speak the truth to others, even in a loving and grace-filled way?

   Think about a situation in which you need to speak the truth in love. How can your group members pray for you and support you as you seek to do this?

7. **Read** Judges 4:11–24. Deborah and Barak were outnumbered, and their enemy had superior armor and weapons. Why were they confident to go into battle even though the odds were against them? What are some of the seemingly insurmountable obstacles you are facing? What will it take for God to overcome them?

8. Satan lies to us and seeks to point out our weaknesses. He does this so we will not boldly follow God and let him work through us. What are some of the lies the enemy tells women (including you)? What specific biblical truth or teaching will help you overcome these lies?

> The greatest enemy we have is Satan, and he is called the father of lies. His tactic is to remind us of what we are NOT instead of whose we ARE.
>
> —*Bianca Juárez Olthoff*

9. Leaders and heroes come in many shapes and sizes. How was each of these people a hero, used by God, and a leader in some way?

  • Barak—

  • Deborah—

  • Jael—

Tell about how one of these three people inspires you to live boldly for God.

10. What is a step of leadership you have been resisting but feel God is moving you to take? How can your group members pray for you and keep you accountable to take the next step for the glory of God?

Satan knows your name, but he calls you by your sin.
God knows your sin, but he calls you by your name.

—*Bianca Juárez Olthoff*

Closing Prayer

Spend time in your group praying in any of the following directions:

- Thank God for the women in your life who have modeled passionate, bold, and humble leadership.

- Invite the Holy Spirit to surprise you with a fresh call to use the gifts he has given you.

- Confess where you have resisted a surprising call of God and commit to do all you can to boldly follow his leading.

- Praise God for the many biblical examples of how he calls people to live and lead for him whom others would have overlooked and left behind.

- Ask God to forgive and change those who have treated you poorly because you are a woman.

- Pray for God's blessing on the women in your life whom God has raised up as leaders to influence you.

You are a child of God, and whatever arena you are in,
he wants to use you.

—*Bianca Juárez Olthoff*

BETWEEN-SESSIONS

Personal Study

SESSION 2

Reflect on the material you have covered during this session by engaging in any or all of the following between-sessions activities. Make a note of any questions or comments that arise from the activities that you would like to discuss at your next group meeting.

Words of Blessing

Make a list of three women God has used to lead, inspire, and influence your life of faith. Then make note of two or three ways each woman has impacted you (seek to be specific):

1. Name: _____

Ways she has impacted, inspired, and influenced me:

-
-
-

2. Name: _____

Ways she has impacted, inspired, and influenced me:

-
-
-

3. Name: _____

Ways she has impacted, inspired, and influenced me:

-

-

-

If some of these women on your list have passed away, or if they are people you have never met but their stories have greatly impacted you, take time to thank God for these women. Celebrate their lives, and praise God for working in them and through them in such beautiful ways.

If some of the women on your list are family members, friends, or people close to you, try to get with them face-to-face to share what God has done in your life through them. Be specific, and let them know how grateful to God you are for them. They will be more blessed than you can imagine.

If others on your list are teachers, leaders, or speakers you have learned from but with whom you have no relationship, consider sending them a letter or email. Seek to look them up online or contact their ministry and find out the best way to get a letter to them. Then prayerfully communicate how God has used their life and ministry to shape your heart and life. They will be thankful you took the time to do this.

Be a Storyteller

Write a short story of a great woman of faith you have known personally. Seek to capture her heart, surprising call, and how God has used her to impact others. Then, if possible, share this story with her and, if she is comfortable with it, look for opportunities to share it with others. You could read it, post it on social media, blog it, or ask others to share the story.

A short story about: _____

_____

_____

_____

_____

_____

_____

_____

Face Your Fears

Make a list of three specific fears you have when it comes to leading others and following God with boldness. Then look up the Bible passages listed below and write how those verses will give you confidence in the future to follow God even when you are feeling cautious. Spend time meditating on these passages.

1. My fear or worry: _____

   Scripture: *"Have I not commanded you? Be strong and courageous. Do not be afraid; do not be discouraged, for the LORD your God will be with you wherever you go"* (Joshua 1:9).

   How this should empower me to follow God:

   Action I can take (with God's help) as I seek to follow him, lead others, and grow bold in my faith:

2. My fear or worry: _____

   Scripture: *"Do not fear, for I am with you; do not be dismayed, for I am your God. I will strengthen you and help you; I will uphold you with my righteous right hand"* (Isaiah 41:10).

   How this should empower me to follow God:

Action I can take (with God's help) as I seek to follow him, lead others, and grow bold in my faith:

3. My fear or worry: _____

Scripture: *"For the Spirit God gave us does not make us timid, but gives us power, love and self-discipline"* (2 Timothy 1:7).

How this should empower me to follow God:

Action I can take (with God's help) as I seek to follow him, lead others, and grow bold in my faith:

Our role as Christians is to lead people to Christ, so by default you're a leader.

—*Bianca Juárez Olthoff*

Journal

Use the space provided on the next page to write some reflections on any of the following topics:

- Record some leadership lessons you have learned from godly women in your life. How can you take these lessons and put them into action?

- Write about some leadership opportunities that are on the horizon. How can you pray for an open heart to be responsive if God calls you to step up as a leader?

- List some of the weaknesses the enemy has pointed out in your life. How can you reject those lies of the enemy and hold on to the truth of God?

Ø Write down specific actions you can take to fortify these areas of weakness and make them areas of strength.

_____

_____

_____

_____

_____

_____

_____

_____

_____

_____

_____

_____

_____

SHULAMITE WOMAN

WE HAD GOD AT HELLO

<u>**Key Scripture:**</u> Song of Songs 1

Lisa Harper

MEETING THE SHULAMITE WOMAN

She was a common young woman who did not see herself as special or extraordinary. As a matter of fact, she had her own insecurities. At one point in her story, the Shulamite woman expressed she did not feel good about how she looked, and she became timid before Solomon, her beloved. Later in her story, she dealt with the fear that she might lose the intimacy and relationship she had with the king. Like many women, she was a mixture of confidence and insecurity. She felt both certainty and fear in her relational world.

The Shulamite woman was a person of great passion. Her words, captured on the pages of Scripture, reveal a depth of love and romantic fervor that would make some people blush. She was articulate and poetic, and entered freely into a powerful conversation with Solomon. Back and forth they expressed with delight their words of affirmation, celebration, and praise.

She was pure. Solomon praised her for protecting herself sexually and saving herself for the covenant of marriage. With all of her beauty, she had restrained herself from being lured into the cultural temptations that exist in every generation. She worked hard and did not seem to wander into the frivolous things of life.

Eventually, the Shulamite woman and Solomon were married, and his celebration of her goodness and beauty was forever recorded in the pages of the Bible. His praise was so effusive that we can hear another voice echoing through his words. We hear the voice of God. In this story, we get glimpses of the gospel of Jesus Christ.

Solomon's praise became a mirror, reflecting the heart and words of God toward his beloved people. The Shulamite woman's words can likewise become a reflection of our praise back to God. If you look closely and listen intently, the love story of Solomon and the Shulamite woman give insight into the story of God's love for you and your love for the One who sees you as precious, beloved, and perfect in his sight.

Introduction

It was a miraculous moment caught on video. What happened was staggering beyond comprehension. Tyrone and Keesha actually ran to get their smartphones so they could record this monumental occurrence. Both mother and father were stunned and amazed when it happened—and delighted they had captured the event digitally. They not only watched the brief video clip over and over, but they also sent it to family members and friends. Those who received and watched it on their phones and computers responded with similar enthusiasm.

Their firstborn son, Will, had learned to pull himself up along the couch in their living room. He had been doing it for a couple of weeks. He even did a little side step to navigate himself from one end of the couch to the other. Tyrone and Keesha sensed that Will might be ready to try taking a few steps on his own. So Tyrone stood him up in the middle of the living room and let Will hold both of his thumbs for balance while Keesha coaxed her son to let go of Daddy and walk to her.

With one hand extended to lure Will toward her, and her phone in the other hand recording this potentially earth-shattering moment, Keesha said, "Walk to Mommy!" Then, it happened. Will let go of Daddy's thumbs, kept his arms straight up in the air, and took four distinct and wobbly steps toward Mommy before he sat down.

Cheers erupted! "What a big boy!" his parents said, lifting him in the air. "You walked, pal! We are so proud of you!" It was time for a celebration.

As you let this scene settle into your mind, remember this: Will did not dance a tango. He did not do a back flip. He did not break an Olympic sprinting record. This little guy simply did what most healthy kids do at about that point in their physical development. He took his first steps and then fell down. That's it!

In response, he was praised and affirmed. The video of this moment was shared with a couple dozen people, as if this moment was a big deal—and as if Will had done something extraordinary.

Why such a fuss over a relatively pedestrian moment? Because little William's parents love him. Every step he takes, each word he speaks, and all the actions of his life will be recorded in their hearts. Tyrone and Keesha affirm, celebrate, and praise him because he is their boy and they love him with deep passion.

In a similar way, our heavenly Father celebrates us. Every step we take, the words we speak, the life we live—they all matter to the God who loves us beyond description and comprehension. When we take a few steps and then stumble, God does not get frustrated or angry with us. He picks us up, gives us a hug, affirms his love, and puts us back on our feet again.

Talk About It

Briefly respond as a group to one of the following questions.

Tell about a time you saw a baby or toddler do something ordinary, and everyone got excited. Why was this moment such a big deal?

Tell about a time you experienced God's fatherly love for you, even when you were not acting perfectly or doing everything just right. How did this make you feel?

"With one glance of your eyes you captured my heart."
Can you imagine God saying that to you?

—*Lisa Harper*

Video Teaching Notes

As you watch the teaching segment for session three, use the following outline to record anything that stands out to you.

The power of songs

Feeling less than perfect

The cost of feeling not good enough

A love story of biblical proportions:

- Solomon and the Shulamite woman

- Jesus and you (another love story)

God's mercy is so much bigger than most of us ever give him credit for.

—Lisa Harper

Small Group Study and Video Discussion

Take a few minutes with your group members to discuss what you just watched and explore these concepts in Scripture.

1. Tell about a song you love that has deep memories in your heart or an interesting story behind it. Why do you think music touches your soul so deeply and certain songs stay locked in your heart and mind for a lifetime?

The Bible reveals God has a favorite tune too. His favorite song is actually a book in the Old Testament, and the formal canonical title for it is the Song of Songs.

—Lisa Harper

2. Tell about a time when someone said or did something that made it clear they were focusing on some part of you that was "imperfect." How did this experience make you feel? What did it do to your soul? (Please share this story without using a name or indicating who it was.)

3. Perhaps you can recall a time in your life when someone made you feel "less than good enough." How do experiences like these impact our heart in the following ways?

   ● How we see and value ourselves . . .

   ● How we see and trust other people . . .

   ● How we see and trust God . . .

What have you found that helps you battle against the lies that can, through such experiences as these, make you feel less than good enough?

That kind of "less than" feeling, that feeling of not being quite good enough, erodes intimacy in human relationships. But how much more so does that impede our relationship with the Lord?

—Lisa Harper

4. **Read** Song of Songs 1:2–4. What do you learn in this passage about the Shulamite woman's honesty in regard to her feelings and her self-confidence?

5. **Read** Song of Songs 1:5–7. The Shulamite woman seems to lose her confidence and boldness in this part of the passage. Tell about a time when you pulled away from another person because you felt insecure or unworthy. What caused you to do this? How did it impact your relationship?

6. **Read** Song of Songs 1:8–10; Romans 8:37–39; Romans 5:8; and Ephesians 2:4–5. Tell about a time when you were amazed by the incredible love of Jesus. How did this impact your faith and life?

7. What are ways you can grow and nurture your sense of intimacy with God and closeness with Jesus? What specific things do you do in the flow of a normal week that helps you grow your intimacy with the Savior?

8. Our culture sends false messages that make us feel we don't measure up, that we will not be good enough until we do certain things, look a certain way, or act differently. What are some of these "if only" statements that many women live with?

What are some of the "if only" statements you *grew up with*?

- If only _____ ,
  I would be lovable and worthwhile.

- If only _____ ,
  I would be lovable and worthwhile.

- If only _____ ,
  I would be lovable and worthwhile.

What are some of the "if only" statements that *still rattle around in your head*?

- If only _____ ,
  I would be lovable and worthwhile.

- If only _____ ,
  I would be lovable and worthwhile.

- If only _____ ,
  I would be lovable and worthwhile.

Share one or two of these with your group and talk about why these lies are so damaging. How can we battle to get rid of this kind of harmful thinking?

9. **Read** John 3:16; 1 John 4:9–11; and 1 John 3:1. We have all heard the old saying, "Beauty is in the eye of the beholder." According to the Bible, how does God behold you?

   What are some ways you experience the love and affirmation of God as you walk through a normal week of your life?

10. What gets in the way of you hearing God's words of affirmation and receiving his extravagant love?

    What can you do to open your ears wider to hear God's words of encouragement and to open your heart more fully to receive the generous love he longs to lavish on you?

This book of the Bible is all about how God loves us just the way we are.

—Lisa Harper

Closing Prayer

Spend time in your group praying in any of the following directions:

◎ Thank God for including a story in the Bible that praises romantic love and the good gift of intimacy.

◎ Give praise to God that this story also captures the greatness of God's love for you and that it gives you a picture of how you can respond back to God with deep praise and affection.

◎ Lift up prayers of praise and celebration for the absolute goodness of God's love for you.

◎ Express your love back to God and tell him how beautiful, precious, and glorious he is to you.

◎ Thank God that he loves you just as you are and that while you were hard-hearted toward him, he loved you and pursued you.

The Song of Songs is the song of all songs, so it is the favorite song on God's iPod.

—*Lisa Harper*

BETWEEN-SESSIONS
Personal Study
SESSION 3

<u>Reflect</u> on the material you have covered during this session by engaging in any or all of the following between-sessions activities. Make a note of any questions or comments that arise from the activities that you would like to discuss at your next group meeting.

Your Heavenly Father

Think about how a loving father and mother delight in a child. Parents get excited about the little things their children do. First steps, first words, and simple signs of growth all become sources of incredible delight.

Now imagine how God sees you as you take little steps of growth on your faith journey. Since he is a perfect Father, you can be confident that he delights even more than an earthly parent. Write down some small steps of faith you have taken over the past year. Be specific about the ways you have grown and moved forward in your faith journey:

Some steps I have taken forward in following Jesus:

What results I have seen because I took these steps of faith:

Some steps I plan to take forward in the upcoming year:

Now, write down some of the ways God delights in you and rejoices in your baby steps forward in faith:

-
-
-
-

A Love Song to My God

The Song of Songs is God's favorite song! In this book of the Bible, we see a real couple express great love for and intimacy with each other. This becomes a picture of God's love for his bride, his people (that means you)! Today, take time to write out your own song of praise to God. Just as Solomon and the Shulamite woman took turns expressing words of affirmation, praise, and celebration, write out your words of blessing to God.

My song of praise to God:

Ways I see your beauty:

How you bring me joy and delight:

How I want my life to bring you joy:

Anything else that is on my heart . . .

A Love Song for Your Beloved

The Song of Songs reminds us that expressions of emotional affection and romantic love are not only acceptable but also encouraged and honoring to God. If you are married or engaged, take time to write down your words of praise, affirmation, and delight in your beloved.

Words to my beloved . . .

Now read these words to your beloved, and let him know what he means to you!

Journal

Use the space provided below to write some reflections on any of the following topics:

- Write down the title of two or three favorite songs from your childhood and a sentence or two about why they mean so much to you.

- Write down what you appreciate about your husband (if you are married). Let these words remind you of what he means in your life.

- Make a list of the many ways God has shown his love to you. Let this remind you of the depth of his love.

RUTH

**STAYING FOCUSED
IN A WORLD OF DISTRACTIONS**

Key Scripture: Ruth 1

Chrystal Evans Hurst

MEETING RUTH

*R*uth might be one of the most unique women we meet in the Bible. She is a bundle of contrasts. She breaks many stereotypes, and her story is both shocking and beautiful.

Ruth lived in one of the most brutal and uncertain times in the story of God's people . . . the time of the judges. This was a period of history when the people of God rebelled again and again and suffered the invasion and dominance of many foreign nations. On top of this, Ruth's story begins in a time of famine and scarcity. Within all of this, Ruth shows herself to be stable and consistent in her pursuit of God and love for people.

Ruth was not an Israelite but a Moabite. She was not an insider but an outsider to God's people. She had married a Israelite man, but he had died and left her a widow at a relatively young age. Then she left her home country and came to a new place, with a new culture, a new people, and a new uncertain future.

Ruth had a gentle and humble heart. At the same time, she had amazing strength and tenacity. She hungered to know more about the God of the Israelite people. Though she was given ample opportunities to stay in her hometown where things were safe and familiar, she committed to follow Naomi, her mother-in-law, into the unknown. More accurately, Ruth was unyielding in her commitment to follow Naomi's God, no matter the cost.

In a startling turn of events, this widowed Moabite woman became the wife of Boaz, an influential leader in Israel. Later, she became the great-grandmother of the nation's most revered and remembered king, David. Even later, she would be found in the genealogy of Jesus Christ, the Messiah and Savior of the world.

When we meet Ruth, we are reminded that anyone can follow God and become part of his plan. To do this, we will have to keep our eyes on the Creator and Savior of our souls and learn to ignore all the distractions and off-ramps that life offers us.

Introduction

Distractions, off-ramps, and the easy way out. We don't always look for these things, but they seem to find us! As we walk through everyday life, we can get off the path God has planned for us without even trying. Before we know it, we veer off the narrow road and find ourselves wandering in places we should have never gone.

Cindy prayed and had a clear conviction that she should go right to college after high school. She knew she wanted to pursue a career in business to use her gift for marketing. Her friends and parents affirmed her direction, and she was committed to this calling. Then the distractions came pounding in. The off-ramps were everywhere. A few of her friends decided to take a year off school to travel, relax, "find themselves," and see the world before they settled into their life plan—and they asked Cindy to join them. Now she felt the pressure. The off-ramp seemed appealing. What should she do?

Rhonda had raised her family, been successful in the family business, and was now retired and an empty nester. She had dreamed about investing significant time in mission work and ministry. She and her husband prayed and decided this next chapter of life was the perfect time to realize their dream. They contacted a couple of great ministries and were ready to volunteer significant amounts of time to serve Jesus as a team. Then, as if on some strange cue, other "opportunities" and "options" came flying at them. Rhonda was offered a new job that paid more than she had ever made before. Friends began talking about taking a cross-country trip with four couples together, which would mean six months of travel and saying no to their plans to volunteer as ministry leaders. What should they do?

Taking time off school is not wrong or sinful. Nor is working a few more years to grow a larger nest egg a bad thing in and of itself. Doing an extended road trip with other retired friends could be a blast! The truth is, many off-ramps and distractions are neutral or even good. The real issue is, *what is the will of God?*

Every Christian who has prayed the familiar words of Jesus, "Your kingdom come, your will be done on earth as it is in heaven," has asked for God's leading. We have declared, "I want your will done in my life!" The real question is, *What is God's will for me?* When we know the answer to that question, we should be careful not to get distracted. We need to avoid all the detours that life offers us.

Talk About It

Briefly respond as a group to one of the following questions.

Tell about a time you had a clear sense of God's leading in a specific area of your life, and then all kinds of off-ramps showed up. How did you respond to these distractions?

What have you discovered that helps you stay on track and on task with God's will for your life, even when there are lots of detours and distractions?

Even good things can get in the way of God things.

—**Chrystal Evans Hurst**

Video Teaching Notes

As you watch the teaching segment for session four, use the following outline to record anything that stands out to you.

A late-night drive in the dark

Decisions over distractions:

● Choose calling over comfort

● Choose reliance over reason

● Seek God's approval over the opinions of others

Decisions lead to destiny

Our decisions lead us to our destiny, but only as much as we avoid the distractions that are bound to come up as we live this life.

—Chrystal Evans Hurst

Small Group Study and Video Discussion

Take a few minutes with your group members to discuss what you just watched and explore these concepts in Scripture.

1. Lots of good things—sometimes *very* good things—can become distractions to the best things God has for your life. Tell about a time you let a "good thing" become more important than a "God thing." How did this affect your life, faith, and sense of following God?

   What are some of the good activities, opportunities, and events you have decided to say no to? How have these choices helped you to follow God's will and stay focused on what matters most in your life?

2. **Read** Ruth 1. What do you learn about the character and heart of Naomi in this story? What do you learn about Ruth's faith, passion, and character?

3. What commitments did Ruth make to Naomi (see Ruth 1:16–18)? What were the implications of those commitments? What were some of the obvious distractions and off-ramps Ruth would have faced that could have moved her off this commitment?

4. Make a list of three commitments or callings that you are confident God wants you to follow and fulfill:

-

-

-

Share one of these with your group members and let them know how they can pray for you, encourage you, and even help you stay on the path to follow God's will in this area of your life.

5. One distraction that can keep us from fully following God's will is the temptation to seek personal comfort over God's calling. How would a decision by Ruth to go home to her parents in Moab have been more comfortable and safer than a decision to follow Naomi to Bethlehem (see Ruth 1:8–10)? What message was Ruth sending when she turned down the opportunity to seek the comfort of home?

6. Think about the commitment or calling you feel God wants you to fulfill (the one you shared with your group in question 4). What distractions and off-ramps, if any, have come along thus far to offer a more comfortable and seemingly safer route for you to travel? How can keeping your eyes on God's call help you resist these distractions?

7. A second lesson we learn from Ruth's story is that we can be distracted from following God's will by relying on our reason more than God's wisdom (see Ruth 1:11–13). How can reason and rational evaluation of a situation get in the way of us following God's plan for our life?

Tell about a time when God called you to follow him that did not make sense from a human perspective. How did God bless your willingness to follow him, even when things did not make sense to you?

8. When you think about the area of calling you shared with your group, what are some of the ways that relying *only* on human reason could get in the way of you fulfilling God's call in this area of your life?

Sometimes we can think our way out of exactly the very place that God wants us to be.

—*Chrystal Evans Hurst*

9. A third common distraction from following God's will is to seek the approval of other people more than the approval of God. How did Ruth's actions show a deep concern for pleasing God more than pleasing people (see Ruth 1:14–18)?

How can the voices, attitudes, and judgment of others get in the way of us following God's plan and will for our lives?

10. Which of the three distractions discussed in this study—choosing comfort over God's calling, following your own reasoning instead of relying on God, and seeking the opinions of others more than God's approval—tends to get your attention quickest and keep it the longest? What steps can you take to resist this distraction?

> *Focus on following God one decision at a time.*
>
> —*Chrystal Evans Hurst*

Closing Prayer

Spend time in your group praying in any of the following directions:

- Thank God for his patience with you, even when life's distractions catch your attention and you take off-ramps from his will.

- Pray for daily power to know and follow God's calling on your life. Also, ask for strength to resist any and all off-ramps.

- Commit to hear and follow God's call, even when it stretches you and makes you uncomfortable.

- Yield your mind to God and commit to use it for his glory. Also commit to surrender your thinking to the lordship of Jesus.

- Ask the Holy Spirit to create a deep and growing desire in your heart to please God above all others.

> *Focus on the One who matters most and trust that, step-by-step, God can and will lead you to the place he wants you to be.*
>
> —*Chrystal Evans Hurst*

BETWEEN-SESSIONS
Personal Study
SESSION 4

Reflect on the material you have covered during this session by engaging in any or all of the following between-sessions activities. Make a note of any questions or comments that arise from the activities that you would like to discuss at your next group meeting.

Planning Your Trip Wisely

Consider the coming year and make a list of two or three areas you feel God is leading you to follow him and be faithful. (This could be in your spiritual growth, how you will serve others, in your relational world, how you will use your finances, or any area of life where you sense God is leading you.) Then write down three key distractions and off-ramps you think you might face as you seek to follow God's plan.

1. God wants me to follow him and be in his will in this area:

   A possible distraction I might face as I seek to follow God in this area:

2. God wants me to follow him and be in his will in this area:

   A possible distraction I might face as I seek to follow God in this area:

3. God wants me to follow him and be in his will in this area:

A possible distraction I might face as I seek to follow God in this area:

Spend time praying for the power of the Holy Spirit to fill you as you seek to avoid distractions and follow God faithfully. Ask one or two of your group members, or some other close Christian friend, to pray for you, keep you accountable, and encourage you as you seek to avoid distractions and follow God with joy and passion.

Getting Uncomfortable

Take time to read, meditate on, and even memorize Matthew 16:24–25:

> *"Whoever wants to be my disciple must deny themselves and take up their cross and follow me. For whoever wants to save their life will lose it, but whoever loses their life for me will find it."*

Now make a list of four comforts you tend to seek that might get in the way of you following God's will for your life with radical commitment:

-

-

-

-

Make a commitment that you will watch for these and avoid them as best you can, in the power of the Holy Spirit.

Being Faithfully Reasonable

Our reason can get in the way of us following God's will for our life. But our reason can also help us identify and follow God's plan. Faith and reason are not enemies—they can function as friends and partners in following Jesus. Today, think and pray about the various ways you sense God is calling you to grow and live more for Jesus. Then come up with three ways you can take bigger steps of faithfulness. When your mind gets in the way, keep following Jesus' will and leading. When your mind can help propel you forward, use it for the glory of God.

One way I know God wants me to grow, surrender, and follow him:

Three ways I can move forward in this area of growth:

-
-
-

If we can silence the distractions, and focus only on the fact that we are called to obey—called to live lives that bring God glory—and move forward in that, I believe we will look back and see that following the call of God was the most important thing.

—*Chrystal Evans Hurst*

Journal

Use the space provided below to write some reflections on any of the following topics:

◎ Write about some of your most common "frivolous" distractions.

◎ Write about some of your most tempting "good" distractions.

◎ List several ways you tend to seek comfort such that it keeps you from following God.

◎ Think about people in your life whose opinions can become too important to you. How can you be sure God's approval matters more to you than the opinions of these people?

PUAH AND SHIPHRAH

HOW TO FIGHT YOUR FEARS

Key Scripture: Exodus 1:15-22

Margaret Feinberg

MEETING PUAH AND SHIPHRAH

*A*s a midwife under the power of the pharaoh of Egypt, Puah worked in tandem with another woman, Shiphrah. Both Puah and Shiphrah were Hebrews, and their occupation was much like that of a midwife today, coming alongside women in the delivery process to help them bring their children into the world. In a prehospital, prepediatrician world, their service was important and needed.

With the growing number of Hebrews and their tendency to multiply, Puah and Shiphrah had a full-time job helping the Hebrew women deliver their sons and daughters. Then the orders came down from on high, from the very throne room of the pharaoh: the women were to kill any boy born to a Hebrew woman. This was the king's way of decreasing the population of Hebrews that was growing rapidly in his land.

Puah and Shiphrah feared God, and they decided that honoring God was more important than obeying an earthly king. So they refused to take the lives of the newborn boys. When the king of Egypt questioned them, they declared the Hebrew women were delivering their own children.

Puah and Shiphrah give us a picture of honoring the King of heaven above any human leader. They are examples of fearlessness in the face of danger and threats. Their story also shows that obedience to God leads to blessing. Their risk-taking spirit inspires us to take chances and be bold in how we live our faith.

Introduction

Anxiety, worry, and fear come in many shapes and sizes today. They come rushing into our lives uninvited, and they never leave on their own accord. They must be driven out, and the door must be locked behind them.

Not only does the world create endless scenarios and reasons for fear, but the enemy of our soul also amplifies and magnifies every one of them. If we are not careful, we will find our hearts and minds ruled by fear rather than faith. If this happens, we will miss countless opportunities to follow God and see him do great things through our lives.

To battle against fear, we need to recognize it, name it, and shine light on it. When we keep fear in the darkness (and fear loves the darkness), it gains power. However, when we illuminate fear with the glorious light of Jesus, it loses power and begins to die. With this in mind, we are wise to search our heart and admit where fear has taken up residence. Then we must decide, in the power of Jesus, to hand fear an eviction notice and point to the door.

What fears do you face today? What worrisome patterns have marked your life for months or years? What patterns of anxiety have become so familiar that you hardly notice they have set up camp in your backyard? It is time to turn on the light of God's truth and watch your fears run for the door. It is eviction time!

This is your moment to battle the power of fear and replace it with bold faith.

Talk About It

Briefly respond as a group to one of the following questions.

Tell about an irrational fear you lived with as a child. How did you finally get over it?

Tell about a fear that God has helped you overcome with his power. How has facing this fear changed your life?

Even when we live in a culture filled with fear, fear doesn't have to reign, because God does!

—Margaret Feinberg

Video Teaching Notes

As you watch the teaching segment for session five, use the following outline to record anything that stands out to you.

The "what if" game . . . don't play it!

Irrational fears and real fears

God's people: from protection and prosperity to oppression and exploitation

Fear God and fear nothing else

The splendid beauty of resisting fear and following God

Three tactics to help you resist the attack of fear:

● Recognize the battle with fear is bigger than you

● Stay your mind on God

● Don't fight fear alone

Practical ideas and tools for overcoming fear

Fear God, and you have nothing else to fear.

—Margaret Feinberg

Small Group Study and Video Discussion

Take a few minutes with your group members to discuss what you just watched and explore these concepts in Scripture.

1. Describe a time you played the "what if" game. Why is this game so dangerous? Why can't we ever win at this game?

2. Tell about a fear you live with today. What are some possible consequences you will face if you let this fear stay camped out in your life and heart?

3. **Read** Exodus 1:8–14. What would it have felt like to be one of the Israelites during this time? How does this movement from protection to persecution seem to be repeating itself through history for those who follow God?

4. How is this passage an example of the truth that fear gives birth to more fear? How have you experienced this troubling reality in your life?

Whenever we allow fear to take root, we create space for worry and anxiety to set up shop in our lives.

—*Margaret Feinberg*

5. **Read** Exodus 1:15–19 and Proverbs 9:10. What does it mean to "fear the Lord"? How can an authentic fear of the Lord free us from fearing other things?

6. Shiphrah and Puah's courage opened the door for the life and work of Moses and also for the coming of the Messiah, Jesus. How might the world have been a different place if Shiphrah and Puah had been paralyzed by fear? How would it have been different if they had failed to courageously resist the plans of the pharaoh?

7. **Read** Isaiah 26:3 and Psalm 27:13. Tell about a time God was present and gave you his *shalom* peace in a situation that could have frozen you with fear. How did keeping your eyes, heart, and mind fixed on God become a conduit of peace in the storm?

8. How can memorizing and reciting Scripture, even one verse over and over, help keep your mind on God and off of the fear-producing lies of the enemy?

If this has been a spiritual discipline you have practiced, how has it strengthened you to fight off the lies of the enemy?

Use the promises of Scripture to stay your mind on God.

—*Margaret Feinberg*

9. Why is it critical for us to talk about our fears with strong Christian brothers and sisters? What are some practical ways we can help each other in times of fear in *each* of the following ways?

● By supporting each other in prayer:

● By offering our presence in hard times:

● By speaking the truth when the enemy speaks lies:

● Other ways we can strengthen each other:

10. <u>**Read**</u> Philippians 4:6–7. What are some practical ways to fight fear that were mentioned during the teaching? How could you use the following tactics to battle a fear you are facing today?

- Deep breathing

- Train your brain

- Specify your prayers

*God invites us to bring all our fears into the light, to him.
By confessing, we shift the focus from the fear to the Father.*

—Margaret Feinberg

Closing Prayer

Spend time in your group praying in any of the following directions:

- Ask God to help you recognize when you are starting to play the "what if" game and pray for strength and wisdom to stop.

- Pray for deliverance from silly and irrational fears. Ask God to help you see them for what they really are.

- If you tend to pull away from others during times of fear, ask God to give you courage to invite others to stand with you.

- Invite the Holy Spirit to turn your eyes toward Jesus and lock your focus on God's power when the fears of life rear their ugly head.

- Thank God for the people he has put in your life who have modeled courage and boldness in the midst of hard times.

If we want shalom, we must pray and ask for it.

—Margaret Feinberg

BETWEEN-SESSIONS
Personal Study
SESSION 5

<u>Reflect</u> on the material you have covered during this session by engaging in any or all of the following between-sessions activities. Make a note of any questions or comments that arise from the activities that you would like to discuss at your next group meeting.

Fighting Fear with Scripture

Consider committing three Bible verses to memory this week. Let these become a source of truth and power when you feel the darkness of fear descending on your mind and life. Begin with these verses:

> Proverbs 29:25: *Fear of man will prove to be a snare, but whoever trusts in the Lord is kept safe.*

> Isaiah 26:3: *You will keep in perfect peace those whose minds are steadfast, because they trust in you.*

> 2 Timothy 1:7: *For the Spirit God gave us does not make us timid, but gives us power, love and self-discipline.*

Find another verse of your choice on the topic of fear and write it in the space below:

Fighting Fear with Friends

Think about one or two women friends in your life who are trustworthy and love Jesus. In the upcoming week, contact them and ask if they would be willing to pray for you and act as an accountability partner as you fight fear in your life. If these women are not in your small group and wonder what moved you to make this request, just share what you have been learning during this Bible study. Invite these women to meet with you and allow you to do the following:

1. *Spend time talking about the fears you are facing*. Share honestly about the fears you are facing. These could be small (and seemingly silly), or they could be deep and based on real issues you are facing. They could be new or longtime fears.

2. *Ask for wisdom*. Invite your friends to share anything they feel the Lord places on their hearts, any Bible passages they believe would help you, or any insights that have helped them overcome fear. This is a powerful way to be part of the body of Christ and share in true community together. Make note of what each person shares with you in the space provided below.

Insights from: _____

Insights from: _____

3. *Ask for accountability*. Share specific ways your friends can encourage you to battle your fears and grow your faith in Jesus. List areas in which you want them to ask you how you are doing and in which they can keep you accountable to do the things that break fear and grow faith.

Specific ways I want to be held accountable:

●

●

●

4. *Pray together.* Agree with your friends that you will be praying for God's power to help you overcome the power of fear in your life. Make a list of specific prayers you will be lifting up before the Lord:

●

●

●

●

Pray together after making the list, and then keep praying in the days to come.

5. *Keep connecting.* Decide how often you will meet with your friends to discuss your areas of accountability, new prayer needs, and how you are experiencing God's help as you grow in faith and flee from fear.

Praying for Persecuted Christians

The people of God were persecuted in ancient Egypt. During the first century, God's people again faced cruel oppression under the Romans, and the persecution continued. Sadly, there are still many of our brothers and sisters around the world who face serious and profound persecution today. In some parts of the world, followers of Jesus are regularly and harshly oppressed.

During the coming week, visit the website for *Voice of the Martyrs* (persecution.com). Every year, the organization provides a global report on where Christians are being persecuted. Open this report, prayerfully review it, and then consider doing the following:

1. Identify one country or region that you will pray for daily during the coming month. Cry out for God's people in this part of the world. Pray for protection, courage, and the powerful presence of the Holy Spirit as you lift up these members of your spiritual family.

Country: _____

Specific Prayer Needs:

-

-

-

-

-

2. Join this ministry in writing letters to your Christian brothers and sisters who have been imprisoned because of their faith.

3. Encourage your small group to adopt a part of the world where persecution is growing, and pray for your brothers and sisters in Christ who live there.

Journal

Use the space provided below to write some reflections on any of the following topics:

- Write down ways God is setting you free from fear and worry.

- Take note of how your faith is growing through this process.

- List your irrational fears and give reasons why you should not heed them.

- List your real fears and describe how it will impact your life if you hold on to these fears and let them grow.

- Write down how your life will become better if you walk in the power of Jesus and leave these fears behind.

_____

_____

_____

ESTHER

LETTING GOD BE IN CONTROL

Key Scriptures: Esther 2–4; 6–7

Courtney Joseph

MEETING ESTHER

*O*f the sixty-six books of the Bible, only two bear the name of a woman: Ruth and Esther. In each case, the woman is a central character in the story and a person of great faith. When we look closely at the story of Esther, we meet a woman who lived through a wide range of experiences and was used by God in stunning and beautiful ways.

To the casual observer, Esther's life can appear to be the story of two radically different women. On the one hand, Esther seems like a pawn on the chessboard of life . . . powerless, abandoned, and oppressed. She suffered the loss of her parents, which would have been deeply painful. She was a foreigner in a land not her own. As a Jewish person in ancient Persia, she would have felt displaced both physically and spiritually.

Esther was also a woman in a time of history and a place in the world where the idea of "women's rights" did not even show up on the cultural radar. To top it off, Esther caught the eye of the king's servants and was taken into the king's harem. Without any say on her part whatsoever, she was placed in a national beauty contest designed to find the king a new queen. She had chosen none of these things for herself and, to a large extent, had not had a say in much of *anything* that had happened in her life up till now. From this vantage point, the casual observer might see Esther as just a victim of the world around her.

But though many things went against her, Esther still had a love and respect for her family. She had a faith in God and a passion to walk in obedience to the Lord's leading. She was willing to stand toe-to-toe and eye-to-eye with Xerxes, the powerful king of Persia, and make a heartfelt appeal for her people. She was able to navigate the political complexities of her day and outsmart the ruthless Persian leader Haman.

For these actions, Esther has become a model of faith and courage for people throughout history.

Was Esther oppressed, abandoned, lonely, and tossed around by the world? Absolutely! Was she strong, bold, faithful, and influential? Yes, she was! What an example for women in every walk of life and in every possible situation. What a woman of God!

Introduction

It's called *black ice*. If you have ever lived in a place where winter hits hard and stays long, you know what this means. If you are from Florida, Southern California, or the Sahara Desert, you may have never even heard of it.

Black ice is a stretch or patch of road that looks normal but has frozen over due to snow, sleet, hail, or other moisture. When weather conditions create this dangerous driving environment, you can be driving along and everything seems fine, and then—all of a sudden—your tires lose traction with the road. Your car begins to drift, slide, and even spin. You feel out of control as your vehicle moves wherever the road takes it.

There is nothing you can do when this happens . . . except pray!

Perhaps you don't live in a cold climate like Fargo or Fairbanks, Buffalo or Boston, and you've never experienced this dangerous and scary situation. But you certainly know the feeling of hitting "black ice" on the journey of life. These are the times your life starts to slide out of control, and you do not even see it coming. Your health is fine one day, and the next something goes very wrong . . . you begin to slide. Your finances are all in order and your future looks secure, then the markets change and a dark cloud begins to form . . . the road becomes treacherous. Your marriage seems solid, and then your spouse, the one who promised, "As long as we both shall live," informs you he's changed his mind . . . things seem out of control.

No one travels long down life's road without hitting "black ice" of some sort. In these moments, you must pray, trust God, and hold tight to the Ruler of the universe.

Talk About It

Briefly respond as a group to one of the following questions.

If you have ever literally hit a patch of black ice, tell what it felt like when your vehicle began to slide out of control. How did this situation turn out?

Tell about a time when you hit "black ice" in some area of your life and knew only God could bring you through. How did God show up and help you during this time?

> *Storms come into every life. No one is immune to them.*
>
> **—Courtney Joseph**

Video Teaching Notes

As you watch the teaching segment for session six, use the following outline to record anything that stands out to you.

Crisis moments . . . we all face them

The story of Esther

Esther did five things:

- She prayed

- She was willing to perish

- She prepared

- She planned

- She was patient

God is in control . . . all the time

An Ephesians 3:20 moment

> *God knows he is your greatest need, and when you have him, you can have faith and courage in the midst of the storm.*
>
> —*Courtney Joseph*

Small Group Study and Video Discussion

Take a few minutes with your group members to discuss what you just watched and explore these concepts in Scripture.

1. During the teaching session, Courtney shared her journey of losing her voice and the lessons she learned from it. What is a journey of loss you walked through with God? What lesson did God teach you through it?

2. One lesson from Esther is that God uses the weak and often unnoticed people of this world to lead and do great things for his glory. What are some of the reasons God loves to use frail, broken, and ordinary people to accomplish his purposes?

How have you seen this to be true in other Bible characters, in the lives of people around you, or in your own life?

> *If God did not use people with weaknesses, he would have no one to use.*
>
> —*Courtney Joseph*

3. **Read** Esther 2–4. (This is a long section of Scripture, but it is a passage that should be heard like a story. Ask for one or two volunteers to do this reading. When Jewish people read this story, they will often "boo" or "hiss" every time the name of Haman is mentioned. You might want to try this. You can even give a little cheer or clap when the names of Esther and Mordecai are read to get into the spirit of the story.) How do you see God in control of what is happening in this part of Esther's story? How is God clearly working behind the scenes?

4. Tell about a time you went through a challenging season and felt God was far away or not listening to your prayers. How were you able to look back later and see that the hand of God was really at work during this time and you did not recognize it?

> *Don't waste an area of pain in your life. It might be the very thing God wants to use for his glory.*
>
> —*Courtney Joseph*

5. **Read** Esther 6–7. (Again, this is a long section of Scripture that needs to be read and heard as a narrative. Feel free to boo and cheer during this reading as well.) Where do you see God's sovereign hand at work orchestrating his will and plan in human history?

6. Tell about a time God called you to do something that seemed strange, countercultural, or had a risk associated with it. How did you follow God's leading, or how did you resist the prompting of the Holy Spirit? How did this situation turn out?

7. Where do you feel out of control in your life right now? What honest and raw questions are floating through your heart and mind as you face this situation?

8. During the teaching, you reviewed five lessons from Esther that can help you walk through the hard times of life when things appear out of control. How can you take one of these practical steps as you face the specific challenge in your life?

   ● How can you *pray* more and specifically for your challenge?

   ● How can you determine you are willing to *perish* (count the cost)?

   ● How can you *prepare* to fight and battle back?

   ● What *plans* do you need to set into place to follow God during this challenging time?

   ● How do you need to be *patient* as you await God's plan to unfold?

   How can your group members pray for you, support you, and encourage you as you stand strong during this painful and difficult time?

> *Whatever you are facing today, you can rest in God's love and care for you. Whatever trial you are in right now is meant to point you to God.*
>
> —*Courtney Joseph*

9. **Read** Ephesians 3:20. What is an example of God doing an "Ephesians 3:20" in your life?

10. What is one situation you are facing right now about which you need to step up and say, "Here I am, Lord, send me"? How can your group members support you and help you to take this bold step of faith?

> *Esther is not the hero of her story, and I am not the hero of mine. God is the hero of every story!*
>
> —*Courtney Joseph*

Closing Prayer

Spend time in your group praying in any of the following directions:

- Thank God that he is on the throne all the time, even when you don't feel it or see it. Declare your trust in his sovereignty.

- Ask God to fill you with courage to follow him and stand for him, even when you feel scared or small.

- Pray for the Holy Spirit to help you navigate the complex situations of life with grace and wisdom.

◎ Give thanks to God for the women he has placed in your life who model deep faith while walking through challenging times.

◎ Pray for the power and wisdom of God to help you through whatever challenges you are facing right now.

From Genesis to Revelation, the Bible tells a story of our God who is in control.

—Courtney Joseph

BETWEEN-SESSIONS

Personal Study

SESSION 6

Reflect on the material you have covered during this session by engaging in any or all of the following between-sessions activities. Make a note of any questions or comments that arise from the activities that you would like to discuss at your next group meeting.

Praying and Fasting in Community

When the pressure was on, Esther called the Jewish people to join her in standing strong. She asked them to fast for her. We can learn from her beautiful example. When we face hard times and feel as if life is out of control, we can ask others to pray for us. We can even ask them to join us in a time of fasting and calling on God to show up, do a miracle, give us strength to stand strong, and lead us through.

Think of three people you know who would gather around you and support you by praying and fasting if you were facing a challenging time. Identify one area in which you need the support of these followers of Jesus:

List several prayer requests you will ask them to lift up:

-

-

-

-

Take time in the coming week to *contact these people.* Share what you are facing and ask if they will partner with you. And remember to follow up and give them an update of how God is moving. Also, ask them to share anything God has placed on their heart as they have been praying and fasting with you.

Make a list of insights they share with you:

-
-
-
-

Look Back, Notice, and Celebrate!

Esther's story reminds us that God is always on the throne and always at work in our lives. Though sometimes we don't see God's hand in the midst of the storm, when we look back, hindsight allows us to see God's fingerprints all over our personal journey. Today, think back over your *past* year and *past decade* to recognize where God was at work.

1. What was a challenging time you walked through in the past *year*?

As you look back, name a few ways you can see that God was present, leading, protecting, providing, and preparing to do something for his glory?

-
-
-

Year after year, the Jewish people remember the story of Esther as they celebrate the Feast of Purim. They stop, look back, remember, and celebrate God's deliverance, sovereignty, and power. In the same way, you can make a decision to praise God and celebrate, in some tangible way, his work in your life as you have gone through challenging times. What are some ways you will celebrate these recent victories?

2. What was a challenging time you walked through in the last *decade* of your life?

As you look back, what are a few ways you can see that God was present, leading, protecting, providing, and preparing to do something for his glory?

-
-
-

How will you celebrate, in some tangible way, God's power and work in your life during that challenging time?

Record Your Ephesians 3:20 Moments

"Now to him who is able to do immeasurably more than all we ask or imagine, according to his power that is at work within us" (Ephesians 3:20).

God will often show up and do far more than we would dare to dream—what we might call "Ephesians 3:20 moments." There is something wonderful about remembering and reflecting on these times God has shown up in power and amazed us with his glory, grace, power, and beauty. So today, write about a time you had an "Ephesians 3:20 moment."

What was your "Ephesians 3:20 moment"? How did God show up in amazing and powerful ways beyond your wildest dreams?

What did you learn about God and his character through this moment?

In what ways has this experience served to increase your faith and trust in God?

In what ways have you used this experience to help others in their faith?

God is in control of my life . . . the good and the bad times.

—*Courtney Joseph*

Journal

Use the space provided on the next page to write some reflections on any of the following topics:

- Write down brief reflections about times when a "black ice" moment became an "Ephesians 3:20 moment."

- Write a personal commitment to give your whole life to Jesus, take up your cross and follow him, and perish for his sake if he were to call you to follow even to the point of death.

- Write a prayer asking God to help you stand strong in the hard times and for eyes to see him at work in the midst of the storm.

PRISCILLA

LIVING A LIFE OF BLESSED ORDINARY

Key Scripture: Acts 18:1–3, 18–26

Karen Ehman

MEETING PRISCILLA

*S*ome biblical characters are flashy, memorable from their mention, and just seem to jump off the pages of Scripture. Their actions are powerful, their words inspirational, and their lives unforgettable. Priscilla was *not* one of these people. This is not to say that God didn't use her powerfully, for he did. But the truth is that, though Priscilla was a faithful and godly woman, she didn't stand out in the crowd. She was someone with whom many ordinary Christians can identify.

Priscilla quietly worked and served Jesus alongside her husband, Aquila. Interestingly, there are places in the Bible where her name is mentioned before her husband's. This is most likely a testimony to her gifting and strong, but humble, leadership in the church and the business world. She and her husband were friends and ministry partners with the apostle Paul. As you read her story, sprinkled through the book of Acts and Paul's letters to the churches, you will discover this woman of faith was generous, wise, and gifted.

In one noteworthy account in Romans 16:3–5, we discover that Priscilla and Aquila risked their lives for the apostle Paul. There is no commentary giving details, and we have no idea what they did to put themselves in harm's way. But there was a boldness and strength in the hearts of this couple. In another situation, Priscilla and Aquila heard a man named Apollos preaching and realized this scholar and gifted communicator did not understand the full message of the gospel. They discreetly took him aside and taught him.

Priscilla's story is not a long narrative. To capture her journey and contribution to the work of Jesus in the first century, we need to bring together short references, snippets, and casual mentions of her name. But when we look at her whole story, we see someone who set a powerful example. She was an ordinary woman who loved Jesus, sought to use her gifts, opened her home graciously, and enjoyed working in partnership with others.

Maybe, at the end of the day, God does more through faithful and ordinary people than through any other group. God made lots of ordinary people. When we let him take our lives in his hands, he can do extraordinary and wonderful things for his glory.

Introduction

On February 26, 1921, a poem was published in an issue of *The Gospel Messenger*. Written by a woman named Myra Brooks Welch to inspire and encourage other Christians, it was a simple reminder that God uses ordinary people in wonderful ways. The message of her poem is needed just as much today as it was back in the early 1920s.

In 1957, this poem became the title of a book by Myra called *The Touch of the Master's Hand*. Then in 1974, a man named John Kramp heard a sermon in which the preacher quoted from Myra's poem and was inspired to turn it into a song. John played the song for the next six years, and it blessed many people. Finally in 1980, John got a call from Wayne Watson asking if he could record this song on his first album. The rest, as they say, is history.

The poem/song is a story about an old violin that is held up at an auction and offered for sale. Because it was old, battered, and out of tune, no one was interested. The auctioneer cried out:

> *One, give me one dollar,*
> *Who'll make it two? Only two dollars, who'll make it three?*
> *Three dollars twice, now that's a good price,*
> *Now who's got a bid for me?*

As the auctioneer tried to sell off this final item—a seemingly worthless violin—for a few bucks, an old man stood up in the back of the crowd and walked to the front. He picked up the violin, dusted it off, and began to play. The melody was, as the song goes, *"Pure and sweet, sweeter than the angels sing."* The auctioneer seized the moment and cried out:

> *One, give me one thousand,*
> *Who'll make it two? Only two thousand, who'll make it three?*
> *Three thousand twice, now that's a good price,*
> *Come on, who's got a bid for me?*

As the price went up, the crowd wondered what had made the dramatic difference in the value of the old, battered instrument? The auctioneer simply smiled and said, *"It was the touch of the Master's hand."*

This poem and song have endured and touched many hearts and lives because the message is true and biblical to the core. When the Master, Jesus, touches a life, ordinary people can be used by God in wonderful and beautiful ways.

Talk About It

Briefly respond as a group to one of the following questions.

Describe a time when you saw someone with great talent or gifting take something that seemed ordinary and make it extraordinary. (This could be ingredients made into a meal, paint and canvas turned into art, words turned into a powerful message, cloth turned into clothing or a quilt, anything at all.)

If you know the poem or song *Touch of the Master's Hand*, talk about how it has inspired or encouraged you. Why do we need messages like this?

All that you have belongs to God.

—*Karen Ehman*

Video Teaching Notes

As you watch the teaching segment for session seven, use the following outline to record anything that stands out to you.

Don't compare yourself to the "exciting" lives of others

Looking at life through the right or wrong lenses

The story of Priscilla, an ordinary life

Work eagerly and diligently

Be gracious and private when you correct others

See your home as a ministry center and share it for God's glory

Open your heart to others

When we view our home through the lens of using it to bring glory to God, it can become a sacred space.

—Karen Ehman

Small Group Study and Video Discussion

Take a few minutes with your group members to discuss what you just watched and explore these concepts in Scripture.

1. Why do you think people spend so much time looking at the lives of others and making comparisons? Why is this dangerous? How can it be discouraging?

2. During the teaching, Karen told the story of how putting on the right glasses brought everything into focus. How do our lives appear different when we look through the lenses of this world instead of through the eyes of God?

   In what ways are you tempted to look at yourself through the lenses of this world? How does this influence how you see yourself?

3. **Read** Acts 18:1–3 and 18:18–26. God brought Aquila, Priscilla, and Paul together during a difficult time in their ministries. What were some of the challenges they were facing? How did this new friendship and ministry partnership become a blessing to them?

   Tell about a person (or a small group of people) God has placed in your life who has become a support network as you seek to live for Jesus. Why do we all need people like this in our lives?

4. God used Priscilla and Aquila to teach Apollos—a man who would go on to influence many other people with the good news of Jesus—about aspects of the Christian faith. Describe some ways God uses people to influence other people who, in turn, go out and have an impact for Jesus in the world. How can you be more intentional and consistent in influencing the people in your life?

Jesus elevated women in his time, often speaking to them when no man normally would.

—*Karen Ehman*

5. **Read** 1 Corinthians 16:19; Romans 16:3–5; and 2 Timothy 4:19. Along with training leaders, running a tent making business, and supporting Paul in his ministry, Aquila and Priscilla led a church that met in their home. How would opening your home as a place of ministry stretch and grow your faith?

What are some ways you are using your home, or could use your home, as a place of ministry?

6. Priscilla's and Aquila's close friendship with the apostle Paul cost them dearly. Apparently, it almost cost them their lives. How can we live sacrificially as we support missionaries, pastors, and people in full-time leadership? What practical steps can you take to support the church leaders God has placed in your life?

7. What is one way you are serving alongside other Christians and using your hands and words to further the work of Jesus? How can your group members pray for you and cheer you on as you share in this ministry partnership?

8. What is one place you sense God might be prompting you to take a new step forward in working alongside someone who is serving Jesus? How can your group members pray for you and keep you accountable to investigate this potential ministry partnership?

9. In today's culture, public criticism and judgment of others seems the norm. How can we emulate Priscilla's example when we need to confront and correct someone? What should we do? What should we avoid?

We can be direct while also being discreet.

—Karen Ehman

10. The relationship between Paul, Aquila, and Priscilla was more than just professional and ministry centered. They had Christian love and affection for each other. Why is it important for us to open our hearts to other believers? What good things might come through these relationships? Why do we avoid them at times?

What are steps you can take to open your heart wider to more people in God's family?

Eagerly work alongside others, using both your hands and your words.

—*Karen Ehman*

Closing Prayer

Spend time in your group praying in any of the following directions:

◎ Thank God for the deep and trusting Christian friendships you have enjoyed over the years. Pray that these relationships will grow even deeper.

◎ Pray that your eyes will be fitted with the lens of Scripture and that you will see the world, other people, and yourself through the eyes of God.

◎ Ask God to help you to be content with however he wants to use you. Offer yourself to him with a commitment to be faithful in both the big things and little things.

◎ Thank God for the people who have instructed, counseled, and even corrected you.

◎ Pray for power to avoid being swept into the comparison game that seems so prevalent in our culture.

If we begin to look at our lives through the lens that God uses, we can view our seemingly ordinary lives in a clearer way, and our calling here on Earth—however mundane it may seem—begins to come into focus.

—*Karen Ehman*

BETWEEN-SESSIONS

Personal Study

SESSION 7

Reflect on the material you have covered during this session by engaging in any or all of the following between-sessions activities. Make a note of any questions or comments that arise from the activities that you would like to discuss at your next group meeting.

Touch of the Master's Hand

Go on YouTube and type in "Touch of the Master's Hand, Wayne Watson." Watch the video and think about how God has worked in your life, with all your struggles, broken places, and hurt. Thank God for loving you and calling you his own, and ask the Holy Spirit to help you see yourself as he does. Also pray for Jesus' power in your life as you seek to serve him each day.

Write down three things God reveals to you during your prayer time:

-
-
-

Now think about a few people in your life who need to be reminded that they are valuable, precious, and loved by God. Send them a link to the "Touch of the Master's Hand" video, and tell them that you see God alive and at work in their lives.

Adjust Your Lenses

Often we see ourselves from the world's perspective because we allow a constant flood of the world's ideas to fill our eyes, mind, and heart, whether via advertising, television and movies, social media, or what we hear other people say. In the coming week, pay attention to the messages you are receiving through these four sources. Track the key messages and record them here:

Messages from advertisements and commercials. What messages are you receiving from this source about who you are and the value—or lack of value—of other people?

-
-
-
-
-

Messages from TV shows, movies, and other kinds of media. What messages are you receiving from these sources about who you are and the value—or lack of value—of other people?

-
-
-
-
-

Messages from social media. What messages are you receiving from this source about who you are and the value—or lack of value—of other people?

-
-
-

-
-

Messages from what other people say. What messages are you receiving from this source about who you are and the value—or lack of value—of other people?

-
-
-
-
-

Stop the Comparisons

Some sources of information, almost by their nature, cause us to compare ourselves to others. We see images, hear stories, and learn about things that make other people's lives seem more meaningful and exciting than our own. Today, identify what causes you to compare yourself to others and feel less valuable. Then cut off that source of information, intentionally, for seven days. This list might include:

- Magazines
- TV shows about beautiful homes, wonderful cooks, successful people, etc.
- Most forms of social media
- Other sources of information that are particularly tempting to you

At the end of seven days, write down how this decision to fast from comparison-inducing stuff has changed how you see yourself and others.

How has my view of others and myself changed during these seven days?

If this exercise has been helpful, try doing it for thirty days . . . or for as long as you like!

Open Your Home

Make a list of ways you could make your home available for some kind of ministry. This could be ministry through your church, ministry to your neighbors, or ministry to your community.

Ways I could use my home for ministry:

-
-
-
-

Choose one of these methods for making your home available for ministry and try it for a season. Maybe for a month. Maybe for three months. At the end of this time, decide if you will continue, or possibly try another idea on your list.

Journal

Use the space provided on the next page to write some reflections on any of the following topics:

- How are you doing at seeing yourself and others in the way that God desires? What are the biblical lenses you should see through?

- Make a list of the Christian people God has placed in your life with whom you have a close friendship. Write down one way you can encourage and bless each of these people.

⊘ Reflect on ways you might be closing your heart to people because of past hurt, betrayal, or bad experiences. Pray and ask God to spare you the folly of missing out on great future relationships because of past hurt.

MARY AND MARTHA

FINDING LIFE IN DEATH

Key Scripture: John 11:1–44

Bianca Juárez Olthoff

MEETING MARY AND MARTHA

*I*f you have been around the church for any length of time, you have most likely heard a sermon, message, or devotional talk about Mary and Martha. In most cases, the message likely focused on how Martha scurried around doing domestic chores while Mary sat at the feet of Jesus and learned from the Master. At the end of the message, you were reminded that Mary chose what was better. This story, and the many sermons it has inspired, focuses on one major difference between Mary and Martha.

However, when we read all the accounts of Mary and Martha, we discover they had quite a lot in common. They were part of a family that loved and served Jesus. Mary, Martha, and their brother, Lazarus, opened their hearts and home to the Savior. When Jesus traveled near Bethany, he would often stay with this family that was so dear to him.

The biblical text paints a picture of deep warmth and friendship between these three siblings and Jesus. When Lazarus was sick and it looked as if he might die, the first thing Mary and Martha did was send for Jesus. The biblical text does not say that Mary sent word, or that Martha sent word—it says, "the sisters sent word." They were a team.

When Jesus delayed and arrived in Bethany after Lazarus had passed away, each of the sisters met with him one-on-one. Their words were very similar, and their faith in Jesus was intact and strong. Martha actually declared, "I know that even now God will give you whatever you ask" (John 11:22). She was confident that Jesus could bring a person back from the dead.

So when you hear the names *Mary* and *Martha*, don't think of Martha as a faithless busybody and Mary as a faithful Jesus follower. Think of two women who were friends of Jesus, who had deep faith in the Savior, and who were close sisters by birth and by faith. Yes, they were unique women of faith, and each had her own spiritual journey and temperament. But they were both confident followers of Jesus.

And they were more alike than you might have been led to believe.

Introduction

What if I was in charge? What if I ran the universe? What if I wrote the script and decided the ending of every story?

Sometimes we face moments in life where crisis crashes in, pain pounds us down, and loss leaves us reeling. In these moments we often find ourselves pondering how the world would work if we were in charge. We might even question God's abilities and wonder if the Maker of the universe is paying close enough attention to our lives.

When we hit these critical moments, we tend to travel down one of two distinct and dramatically different paths. The first path is to question God, focus on the pain, and grow bitter. During these times we think God must not care or have the power to fix our situation. We don't see the hope of resurrection but only the darkness of the tomb. No follower of Jesus wants to walk down this path of doubt and fear, but it is wide and well worn. It is easy traveling.

The second path is harder to find. This road demands that we hold the hand of Jesus and let him lead us, even when we are in pain and struggling with doubt. This path of confident faith is narrow and sometimes drenched with tears. But when we travel it, we walk in hope, anticipation of God's glory, and confidence that the resurrection power of Jesus is available to us.

Every Christian will come to a fork in the road (many times). We will receive bad news, face deep loss, or enter a time of suffering. The question is not whether we *will* face hard times, but *what road* we will take when the pain and sorrow come descending into our lives.

We can take the hand of Jesus when the path seems dark. We can commit to trust God even when we do not understand his ways. We can cry out for the power of the Holy Spirit when we feel weak and empty. When we do, we find the strength we need to press on and walk with Jesus through the storm and out the other side with our faith stronger than ever.

Talk About It

Briefly respond as a group to one of the following questions.

Tell about a time you received some unexpected bad news. How did you respond? How did your faith in Jesus factor into this response?

Tell about a time you found yourself running from Jesus during a hard time rather than clinging tightly to his hand. What was the result of your decision?

You can believe that God is working all things out for the good of those who believe in him, even in the middle of the mess.

—Bianca Juárez Olthoff

Video Teaching Notes

As you watch the teaching segment for session eight, use the following outline to record anything that stands out to you.

Two stories of crisis . . . one small and one big

Discipleship: when we go through a time of "death"

Jesus' shocking response to Mary and Martha

Can you heal? Are you able? Are you good?

The real pain Mary and Martha felt

Jesus is the resurrection . . . in all things

Where am I experiencing a kind of death?

You can worship God because he is good, he is able, and he can bring back to life that which is dead.

—Bianca Juárez Olthoff

Small Group Study and Video Discussion

Take a few minutes with your group members to discuss what you just watched and explore these concepts in Scripture.

1. What is your knee-jerk response when you experience loss, pain, or bad news (in your life or the life of someone you love)? How has your response to bad news and suffering changed during the time you have been a follower of Jesus?

2. There are many kinds of death we can face: death of a dream, death of a marriage, death of a child, death of hope, and many more. Tell about one way you are facing the pain and uncertainty of some kind of death. How have you been responding to this challenging situation?

3. **Read** John 11:1–7, 14, 17–37. How do you think Mary and Martha felt when they first sent word to Jesus? What did they expect? How do you think they felt when Jesus did not show up in time and their brother died?

4. Mary and Martha were real people with deep faith *and* genuine doubts. What do you learn about their faith in this passage? What do you learn about their struggles and doubts?

5. **Read** John 11:4–7. Why was Jesus' response to the news about Lazarus so shocking? Name a time in your life when God's response to your prayer was confusing and hard for you to understand.

6. We live with pain avoidance and a natural aversion to suffering of any kind. If we were to write the script, we would make sure the ending read "happily ever after" and that it would happen as soon as possible. Think back over your life and reflect on a time of hardship that you would have ended quickly if you were in charge of the universe. How did God use the long journey of struggle and pain to do a work in you or others that never would have happened if the process had been cut short?

7. **Read** Matthew 16:24–25. Too many Christians see God as a genie in a bottle, a heavenly Santa Claus, or a lucky rabbit's foot. How do Jesus' words in this passage battle against these images that reduce God to something we control? What are practical ways we can live as those who do each of these things daily?

- Deny ourselves

- Take up the cross

- Follow Jesus

He is God, but he is not a genie who we rub and caress to obtain our wanton wishes.

—Bianca Juárez Olthoff

8. One way we can keep following Jesus in the midst of confusion, chaos, and even catastrophe is to declare what we know to be true. What do *each* of these mean, and why is it healthy for us to declare them?

- "I believe God is able!"

- "I believe God is powerful!"

- "I believe God is good!"

9. God *is* good, and he is able to do all things. The challenge is that God does not always behave as we think he should. His timing is not our timing, and his ways are not our ways. What helps you keep following God even when he does not answer prayers as you want? What do you know about who God is that helps you stand strong?

10. Mary fell at the feet of Jesus. She yielded and submitted even when things did not make sense to her. What are ways you need to bow down, submit, and surrender more fully to Jesus? How can your group members pray for you and help you in your desire to live a more surrendered life before the Savior?

The cost of discipleship is that it will cost you everything. But most importantly, it will solidify and strengthen your faith.

—Bianca Juárez Olthoff

Closing Prayer

Spend time in your group praying in any of the following directions:

- Thank God that he is wiser than you and that his ways are always perfect, even when you don't understand them.

- Pray for those you love who are facing storms and struggles in life. Ask God to help them see his face, even when the storm rages on.

- Invite the Holy Spirit to grow your ability to accept God's ways, even when they seem strange and confusing to you.

- Praise Jesus for his resurrection and ask for eyes to see his resurrected presence with you every day.

- Ask God to teach you patience to wait on his answer to prayer rather than become frustrated when he does not do what you want in the timing you expect.

To be a disciple of Christ, you may not know the WHY, but you know the WHO.

—Bianca Juárez Olthoff

BETWEEN-SESSIONS

Personal Study

SESSION 8

Reflect on the material you have covered during this session by engaging in any or all of the following between-sessions activities. Make a note of any questions or comments that arise from the activities that you would like to discuss at your next group meeting.

Partners in Waiting

We all have friends and loved ones who are going through times of pain, loss, and struggle. In these seasons of life, they are often praying and waiting. Waiting and praying. They can feel very alone and sometimes abandoned. Today, identify someone in your life who is going through a time like this. Commit to do the following things as you become a partner in waiting:

1. *Pray for them*: Make a point of lifting up their needs on a regular basis . . . daily if possible, but at least weekly.

2. *Pray with them*: Get face-to-face, talk online, or communicate by phone. Pray with them at least once a week as they walk through this season.

3. *Communicate with them*: Drop them a note, email, or text and remind them of your love and prayers, and of God's presence and love.

4. *Sit with them*: Spend time with them and simply be a friend. Listen, encourage, talk, and laugh, but don't feel you have to have all the answers . . . because you don't.

5. *Read Scripture with them*: Choose appropriate psalms, read from the Gospels, and ask what Bible passages they love. After reading, talk about what God is saying to both of you.

6. *Don't try to defend or explain God*: Remember, God is God, and we are not.

God Is Good

It is always important for us to remember that *God is good*. When we walk through hard times, memories of God's faithfulness, presence, and power in the past give us hope for the future. Make a list of ten specific ways God has been good to you. Read this list often and reflect on all God has done in the past. Here are some prompts to get your list of thankfulness going:

◉ How God has been good in putting wonderful people in your life

◉ How God has protected you in the past

◉ How God has provided things you needed in surprising ways

◉ How God has lavished spiritual blessings on you, including the love of his only Son, Jesus

Ten ways that God has been good to me:

1.

2.

3.

4.

5.

6.

7.

8.

9.

10.

When you lay down that thing that is bitter or that thing you want in a posture of worship at the feet of Jesus, something changes.

—Bianca Juárez Olthoff

The Road to Discipleship

Jesus was crystal clear about what it means to follow him. What was true two thousand years ago is just as true today. Write down three specific implications for your life if you are going to do each of the things Jesus calls you to do:

If I am going to *deny myself*, I will need to:

*

*

*

If I am going to *take up my cross*, I will need to:

*

*

*

If I am going to *follow Jesus*, I will need to:

*

*

*

As you pray through this list, decide which of these actions you need to take and ask God for power to follow him in a fresh new way. Then take action and live out your faith.

Journal

Use the space provided below to write some reflections on any of the following topics:

- Make a list of "deaths" you have faced and how God has shown up with resurrection power in the midst of these painful times.

- How are you tempted to treat God like a genie in the bottle? Write a prayer of confession and ask God for power to submit to him rather than seeking to control him.

- Write out who Jesus is to you. Express why you can trust his character over your circumstances.

BENT WOMAN

**WE'VE GOT GOD'S
COMPLETE ATTENTION**

<u>**Key Scripture:**</u> Luke 13:10–17

Lisa Harper

MEETING THE BENT WOMAN

Have you ever known someone for a long time and still had a strange sense that you never really got past the surface to the heart of that person? Some people build walls and wear masks. For one reason or another, they are guarded and don't reveal who they really are.

There are also people we encounter who open their heart and life so wide that we feel as if we know them in the first ten minutes. Their story is clear to see, and they wear their heart on their sleeve. No walls, no masks, no pretense. Just authentic and honest living.

We never learn the name of the bent over woman in Luke 13, but she bares her soul and shares her story powerfully. Her encounter with Jesus lasted just a few moments and takes up only eight verses in the Bible, but the lessons we learn from her can last a lifetime.

She was a daughter of Abraham, which means she was Jewish by birth and blood. This identity as a daughter of Abraham—and more importantly as a child of God—was core to how she saw herself. But that was not her whole story. The woman was under demonic oppression. For almost two decades, she had been tormented by the enemy. Day after day, month after month, year after year, she had felt the weight of hell's attacks.

This spiritual attack was so heavy that it literally bent her over and made her physically crippled. This one–two punch of physical and spiritual bondage had dominated her whole life. Yet even with this oppression, she boldly attended the synagogue to meet Jesus, who was teaching that particular day.

When his eyes fell on her, everything changed. What was broken was healed. What was oppressed was delivered. What was bent became straight. Her whole life was transformed. When Jesus saw her, invited her close, and healed her, a new life began.

We don't know her name but only her story. Yet if we are honest, it is our story. We come to Jesus bent, broken, captive, and needy. Jesus sees us, heals us, and straightens out our bent lives. When this happens, we are given a new name: *daughter of the living God.*

Introduction

A mom is sitting at her desk, savoring a few minutes of quiet and serenity. She has just battled with a toddler and newborn who failed to embrace their need for an afternoon nap. After forty-five minutes of rocking, feeding, singing, praying, and begging, they have finally dozed off. Now she has fired up her computer to check a few messages and do a little correspondence before the kids wake up—and the whirlwind begins again.

Out of the corner of her eye, she sees a small figure standing at the door of the living room. She does not even look. She knows . . . he is up already. The full nap lasted about seven minutes. Her toddler is not interested in staying in bed. He is not tired. He wants Mom's attention.

Her body tenses up. She says a quick prayer for patience. She knows this little window of peace is the only chance she will have to communicate with the outside world. She sits silently and does not make eye contact. She hopes against all hope that maybe he will just quietly go back to bed and sleep for an hour or so.

Then the words come. They are not spoken in a demanding way but with honest gentleness. "Mommy, I need . . . "

Let's play a fun little game called, "How will this scenario end?" Here are three options:

1. "Billy, get back in bed. You have only been down for seven minutes. Mommy needs time for herself. You know you are not supposed to get out of your bed during nap time. I don't want to see you or hear from you until I say you can get out of bed."

2. "Billy, Mommy loves you, but nap time is not over yet. Let's go back to your room together, and we can talk about why it is important for you to get a good nap."

3. "Billy, I love you. I missed you while you were asleep. Come give me a hug and let's talk."

Talk About It

Briefly respond as a group to one of the following questions.

If you were "Mommy" in this story, how would you respond to this "interruption" to your limited alone time in the day?

What is your natural and knee-jerk response when someone interrupts you while you are seeking to get a little time to yourself?

Jesus never considers us to be an interruption or a bother.
We are always a delight to him.

—*Lisa Harper*

Video Teaching Notes

As you watch the teaching segment for session nine, use the following outline to record anything that stands out to you.

When tragedy strikes

A humorous interruption

A serious interruption to Jesus' final synagogue sermon

Jesus confronts the religious leaders

The culture of the day and how surprising this encounter really was

Jesus, an example of how to respond to "interruptions"

God is watching you . . . what do you think he feels as he looks at you?

Jesus beckons you closer. You do not have to be bent by anything or anyone anymore.

—Lisa Harper

Small Group Study and Video Discussion

Take a few minutes with your group members to discuss what you just watched and explore these concepts in Scripture.

1. During the teaching session, Lisa tells the story of wandering into a men's restroom by accident and "interrupting" the men. Tell about a time you accidentally interrupted someone. How did you feel? What was the response of the people you interrupted?

2. **Read** Luke 13:10–13. In the context of the story, it is clear this woman meant to interrupt this group of men and Jesus in particular. How did this woman's encounter with the Savior break the social conventions of the day? How was Jesus' response also a breach of the social norms of the day?

3. This woman was sick and tired of being sick and tired. She came to a point of personal desperation where she simply had to cry out to Jesus. In the same way, we all hit times when we are sick and tired of being sick and tired of a certain life struggle. What situation are you facing right now that you are weary of and need the help of Jesus? How can you and your group members pray together and cry out to heaven for the Savior's touch?

4. **Read** Luke 13:14–17. What conflict do you see develop in this passage? Why is Jesus so hard on the religious leaders? What did Jesus see that they missed?

5. Jesus is in the business of making bent people whole and setting spiritual captives free. The religious leaders, however, seemed more interested in following rules and regulations. What are ways we can miss God's healing, love, and grace because we are focused on following rules instead of letting Jesus touch us? What are ways that other people (even well-meaning religious people) can get in the way of us receiving the amazing healing grace of the Savior?

People who are more concerned about religiosity than they are about relationship with Jesus tend to be occupied with rules instead of liberty.

—Lisa Harper

6. Tell about a time you broke a social convention or norm because God was calling you to something bigger or better. How did your holy rebellion turn out?

7. The woman in this story had not stood up straight for almost *two decades*. In what ways do you think eighteen years of brokenness impacted her life, physically and otherwise? How do you think her life changed after Jesus touched and healed her?

What are one or two ways your life has changed (bent things growing straight) since you allowed Jesus to touch, deliver, and heal you?

8. Knowing Jesus as our Savior is incredible. Our sins are washed away, and heaven is our new destination. Embracing Jesus as the One who liberates us from bondage and heals us of our brokenness changes every moment of every day of our lives. What's the difference between just knowing Jesus as Savior and experiencing him as the Liberator of your life? How is Jesus liberating you? What is he setting you free from?

Some people know Jesus as their Savior but not as their Liberator.

—Lisa Harper

9. During the teaching, Lisa told about how her daughter has become a living picture of God's grace and love. What situation or person has God used to show you his love and grace, even in your brokenness?

10. Tell about a personal experience of suffering and pain that lasted a long time. How did the journey of struggle or suffering impact your faith? If you are still in the middle of it, what is helping you stand strong? How can your group members help and support you through this time of need?

God wants all of us to stand up to our full spiritual height. Not to just be saved from our sins but to actually live the abundant, exuberant life.

—*Lisa Harper*

Closing Prayer

Spend time in your group praying in any of the following directions:

◎ Thank God that when you draw near to him he always waves you closer, touches you, and brings his healing power.

◎ Pray for courage to know that you can "interrupt" God any time. Ask him to help you know that you are never an interruption.

◎ Ask the Holy Spirit to give you eyes to see people who are bent over emotionally and spiritually and pray for courage to minister to them.

◎ Lift up the needs of your group members and ask for God's healing and grace to flood their lives.

◎ Pray for someone you love and care about who has still not come to Jesus for his healing touch and grace. Pray that this person will know he or she can draw near to Jesus and experience the healing that only he can give.

If you will turn toward Jesus, he will never say, "Hang on a minute, this isn't a very convenient time for me." Instead, he will always beckon you closer.

—*Lisa Harper*

BETWEEN-SESSIONS
Personal Study
SESSION 9

<u>Reflect</u> on the material you have covered during this session by engaging in any or all of the following between-sessions activities. Make a note of any questions or comments that arise from the activities that you would like to discuss at your next group meeting.

Help on the Long Journey

Think of three people you care about who are "bent over" beneath the weight of deep struggle and pain, whether financial, relational, emotional, physical, or spiritual. In the space below, write down the weight that is burdening each individual.

1. Name: _____

   What weight is pushing down and burdening this person?

2. Name: _____

   What weight is pushing down and burdening this person?

3. Name: _____

   What weight is pushing down and burdening this person?

Take time in the coming weeks to help one or more of these people in some of the following ways:

1. *Pray for God to deliver the person.* Ask the Holy Spirit to help this person sense the gentle eyes and tender touch of Jesus and to draw close to him however difficult the situation.

2. *Pray with this person.* Find time to get with this person face-to-face, over the phone, or online. Spend time praying for God's care, comfort, healing, deliverance, and grace to flood his or her life.

3. *Share what you learned in this session.* You might want to watch the video segment with the person, review some questions in the study guide, and talk about Jesus' power to deliver.

4. *Offer help.* Offer to help in any practical way that might lift a bit of the burden the person is feeling.

5. *Offer words of encouragement.* Write or speak words of blessing and encouragement to this person on a regular basis.

6. *Share Scripture.* Share one or two passages from the Bible that you feel might bring the person hope and joy in the middle of his or her journey.

The Gospel and "Interruptions"

Each of the Gospels—Matthew, Mark, Luke, and John—contain examples of times when people "interrupted" Jesus as he was traveling, doing ministry, or living life. Take time this week to read each of the passages below. Then write down some lessons you learn about how Jesus dealt with those people who "interrupted" him.

Passage	The interruption	What you learn from Jesus' response
Matthew 19:13–15		
Mark 2:1–12		
Luke 18:35–43		
John 12:1–11		

Make a list of the three biggest lessons you learn from these examples of how Jesus responded when people "interrupted" him:

1.

2.

3.

Now make a list of the three ways you want to respond when people "interrupt" you in the flow of your day. How will you seek to live in the light of what you learn from Jesus?

1.

2.

3.

Rejoicing in the Liberty and Freedom of Jesus

When you are walking alongside someone who experiences God's delivering power, commit to celebrate. When someone you care about feels the healing touch of Jesus in any area of life, take time to have a party or rejoice in some other way. Make celebration normative and noticeable.

Make a list of four specific ways you can celebrate moments when grace pours out, healing comes, and deliverance is experienced:

1.

2.

3.

4.

Our past does not impede our glorious future. If you are a child of the Most High King, if you have put your hope in Jesus, stand up, stand up, stand up!

—**Lisa Harper**

Journal

Use the space provided below to write some reflections on any of the following topics:

- Write down what you think your heavenly Father sees when he looks at you.

- Write down what you think God might say about you as you walk through a normal day.

- List some ways you can grow in your understanding and acceptance of the fact that God loves you deeply, is always glad to engage with you, and delights in you as his beloved child.

WOMAN WITH THE ISSUE OF BLOOD

WHEN PERSISTENCE PAYS OFF

<u>Key Scripture:</u> Luke 8:43–48

Chrystal Evans Hurst

MEETING THE WOMAN WITH THE ISSUE OF BLOOD

*C*haracter is often formed in the furnace of suffering. Strength is tested as the storms of life pound against our soul. Faith grows when we hold to Jesus during the dark times. The woman we meet today is an example of character, strength, and faith. She suffered with an illness that assaulted her body for more than twelve years. Just think about this. What were you doing twelve years ago? How much has your life changed in the last decade?

This woman bled for *twelve years*. Due to religious rules and cultural norms, her illness made it impossible for her to take part in social or religious life. She was an outcast, set on the sidelines of society. But she did not spend those twelve years passively waiting. She had done all she could to receive healing, but it had not come. So, when she heard that Jesus would be traveling near her hometown, she decided to do the unthinkable.

This woman had faith that Jesus could heal her, but she knew she was unclean. As a result, she could not touch anyone without making that person unclean. She had avoided touching people for so long, but on this day, she was ready to reach out to someone. And not just anyone—she was going to touch the Rabbi, Jesus. When she did, she was immediately healed. What seemed like a lifetime of bleeding, loneliness, and social isolation was finally over!

Her hope at this point was to quietly melt away into the crowd and start her new life. Her plan was to touch Christ, be healed, and not be noticed. But when the healing went out from Jesus, he stopped and looked at the mass of people pressing around him. "Who touched me?" he asked. His disciples pointed out the obvious—*everyone* was touching him. Jesus clarified that someone had been healed and asked the person to identify themselves.

The woman spoke the truth. She had reached out and broken social norms. An unclean woman had touched the Rabbi. Jesus did not scold her, but declared, "Daughter, your faith has healed you. Go in peace."

Who was this woman? Jesus said it best. She was a daughter. She was healed. She found peace!

Introduction

Sometimes the road is long and hard, and it seems like the end is nowhere in sight.

Ellen stood before friends, family, and God as she said, "For better, for worse." The first nine years of her marriage seemed to be marked by the "for worse" part of her vows. Her husband, Lance, was a hard worker and a good provider, but he never seemed to have anything positive or kind to say. He was critical and detached emotionally. Ellen longed for him to show some tenderness and to engage in caring conversation, but he seemed unable or uninterested. As she approached year ten, she asked God, "Lord, is there any hope things will change?"

Renata had been active and athletic during her school years and into her early twenties. She loved running, water skiing, and hiking. Then out of nowhere, she began to feel strange pains in her body that she had never felt before—first in her knees, then in her back, and finally in her neck. For the next five years she visited five different specialists, but no one could identify the cause or provide a cure. During this half decade, Renata had to stop her athletic endeavors. On top of losing the joy of engaging in outdoor activities, her new sedentary lifestyle caused her to gain twenty pounds. She was discouraged and, at times, depressed.

Holly worked hard to earn a college degree. She did not come from a wealthy family, so she had to take out loans to pay for her education. After college she started looking for a job, but no one seemed to be in the market for a first-year teacher. For two school years she applied to every district in her area and did substitute teaching, but still no one hired her for a full-time job. She started working at a local coffee shop to make ends meet, but she did not earn enough to pay back her student loans, bills, and rent. By the third year after graduation, Holly started going through the same process of applications, phone calls, and making contacts with everyone she knew in the school systems. Sadly, it looked like another school year might start without a teaching job.

Talk About It

Briefly respond as a group to one of the following questions.

Tell about a time you had to persist through a long season of waiting and struggle. What was the most difficult part of that time in your life?

Why is it hard to be hopeful when times are hard, life is painful, and the future seems unpredictable? What gives you hope during these seasons of life?

God can be trusted. He is worth pursuing.

—Chrystal Evans Hurst

Video Teaching Notes

As you watch the teaching segment for session ten, use the following outline to record anything that stands out to you.

Problems . . . we all face them

Persistence . . . we all need it

- Natural persistence

- Supernatural persistence

- Personal persistence

Proclamation (the point of persistence)

How can you connect your situation with your Savior?

When I am tempted to give up, I remember the lives of those close to me, many of whom have experienced the glory of God shining brightest in their life in the darkest of times.

—Chrystal Evans Hurst

Small Group Study and Video Discussion

Take a few minutes with your group members to discuss what you just watched and explore these concepts in Scripture.

1. How have you experienced the presence and tender care of God during a long season of struggle and pain?

2. We all have times when we grow weary of pressing on and pushing through the pain this world can bring. What is one life situation that you're trying to push through right now?

> *It is often in the midst of our choice to hope in God that God shows up and moves in our circumstances.*
>
> —*Chrystal Evans Hurst*

3. God often calls us to do our part when it comes to meeting our needs. When you think about the area of life in which you are growing weary of pressing through, what do you feel God wants you to do? What part are you already doing? What do you need to start doing right away?

4. **Read** Luke 8:43–48. The woman in this encounter was severely limited by the problem she faced. She could not go into the place of worship and touch other people, and she was considered an outcast. Her struggle had spiritual, physical, emotional, financial, and relational implications. What are some of the implications and consequences of the challenge you are facing? How can your group members support you in prayer and in action?

5. The woman in this story persisted. She would not give up! For more than a decade she did all she could to get better. What are some ways you have persisted while walking through your challenges? What is one way you need to start persisting or to persist with greater tenacity as you hold to Jesus in the midst of your storm?

6. Having a plan for persistence is essential. We need to be specific, practical, and detailed.

Think about these examples:

A woman is dealing with health issues, and her doctor says that daily exercise and a healthier eating plan would help the healing process. What are three practical actions she could take that would help accomplish this goal?

-
-
-

A woman has been struggling with financial debt and money challenges for a long time. She knows that if she could adjust her standard of living and get debt-free, she would have far less stress in her life. What are three practical actions she could take that would help accomplish this goal?

-
-
-

What are three things you can do to partner with God in pressing through your challenge?

-
-
-

Share your action plan with your group and ask for their encouragement and prayers.

Be willing to do what you can with what you have.

—*Chrystal Evans Hurst*

7. Our persistence, planning, and efforts can only go so far. We also need *spiritual* persistence. Talk about practical ways you can persist in the following areas of your spiritual life and explain how you believe each will strengthen you as you persist:

● Regular reading of Scripture

● Regular time in prayer

● Regular time worshiping God in song and praise

● Regular time in fellowship with other believers

8. Why is it essential for us to not only do our part to draw near to God and make a plan to persist but also trust God that he can bring us through our struggle?

What is the danger if we do our part but don't trust God to do his part? What is the danger if we trust in God but don't do our part and take action?

9. Jesus did not let the woman touch him, receive healing, and then sneak away. He called her out and asked her to identify herself. Why do you think Jesus wanted the woman to encounter him face-to-face and acknowledge her healing? What was Jesus asking her to do and proclaim?

10. **Read** Ephesians 1:3, 18–23. The woman with the issue of blood would have been happy with simple healing, but she received many more blessings from Christ. What have you received from Jesus that is a clear sign of his love and his over-and-above blessings?

Our persistence matters. There's always more available when we pursue Jesus.

—*Chrystal Evans Hurst*

Closing Prayer

Spend time in your group praying in any of the following directions:

- Thank God for being with you and never leaving you, even through the long seasons of pain and struggle.

- Pray for power to stand strong and see the face of Jesus no matter what you face in this life.

- Pray for one of the other people in your group who is seeking to persist and stand strong in her time of suffering.

- Invite God to give you wisdom to make practical plans to persist through the hard times of life.

- Ask God for healing, freedom, and deliverance from whatever pain and loss you are facing today.

- Commit to hold the hand of Jesus no matter what you face, and ask God for spiritual perseverance as you grow in faith, even in hard times.

The woman with the issue of blood was persistent in the natural, but what got her healing was her persistence in the supernatural.

—*Chrystal Evans Hurst*

BETWEEN-SESSIONS
Personal Study
SESSION 10

<u>Reflect</u> on the material you have covered during this session by engaging in any or all of the following between-sessions activities. Make a note of any questions or comments that arise from the activities that you would like to discuss at your next group meeting.

Fill Your Heart and Mind

As you persist during hard times, one of the best things you can do is to meditate on the truth of God's Word. In the next few days, memorize the following three passages on persevering through trials. Then when you are struggling and feeling discouraged, let the truth and words of these passages run through your mind and heart.

> Romans 5:3–4: *We also glory in our sufferings, because we know that suffering produces perseverance; perseverance, character; and character, hope.*

> Hebrews 12:1–2: *Let us run with perseverance the race marked out for us, fixing our eyes on Jesus, the pioneer and perfecter of faith.*

> James 1:12: *Blessed is the one who perseveres under trial because, having stood the test, that person will receive the crown of life that the Lord has promised to those who love him.*

Now find a key passage of Scripture that relates to the specific struggle you are facing. Just go to Google or some other search engine and type in something like: "Best Bible passages about patience in physical suffering," "best Bible passages about financial struggles," "best Bible passages about conflict resolution," or whatever relates to your area of struggle. Choose your passage and write it below.

Once you have committed this verse to memory, think about adding one or two more.

Planning for Proclamation

Jesus wants us to proclaim his goodness, healing, and glory. To do this, we need to be ready to articulate and express the amazing things he has done. So today, write out a personal proclamation of two different life experiences:

1. *My proclamation of a time Jesus healed, delivered, or helped me through a hard time in life.* Write out what you faced, how Jesus showed up and moved, and how this has changed your life:

2. *My proclamation of when I became a follower of Jesus.* Write out what you were like before you became a Christian, and how the forgiveness and grace of Jesus has changed your life:

Take time to read and practice sharing these stories. Tell them to other believers and even to non-believers.

My Plan for Spiritual Persistence

In this session, you began thinking about making a plan for spiritual persistence. Now, take an extended period of time to work on a personal plan for spiritual persistence that can help you in every time of life. Write personal goals and commitments in each of the following areas:

● Regular reading of Scripture:

● Regular time in prayer:

● Regular time worshiping God in song and praise:

● Regular time in fellowship with other believers:

● Development of other spiritual disciplines:

Share your commitments with one or two trusted Christians and ask for their prayers and encouragement. Also invite them to keep you accountable.

Journal

Use the space provided below to write some reflections on any of the following topics:

Keep a list of forward steps and areas of growth in your spiritual disciplines over the coming months.

Write down different ways God is growing your heart and mind as you memorize and meditate on the truth of the Bible.

Jesus called the woman in this passage "Daughter." He affirmed her faith. He declared her healed. What are some of the ways Jesus has blessed you and spoken life and love to you?

ELIZABETH

HOW TO WIN THE WAITING GAME

Key Scripture: Luke 1:1–45

Margaret Feinberg

MEETING ELIZABETH

They must have looked like the perfect couple. Zechariah was a priest, and priestly blood coursed through his views. His wife, Elizabeth, was also a descendant of Aaron, the first high priest of Israel. From a spiritual perspective their pedigree was impeccable, and both were passionate servants of God and righteous in his eyes. They followed the commandments of the Scriptures and the regulations of the Law to the smallest detail. They had lived a long and full life and were greatly respected and honored in the Jewish community.

Elizabeth's life can look picture-perfect at first glace and from a distance. But if we look more closely, we discover she had become an expert in waiting. In her culture and day, having children was a sign of God's blessing on and presence in your life. Elizabeth had so much, but she was still missing something. She longed to be a mother, to bear children, to experience this unique "blessing" of God.

At this point in Elizabeth's life, the waiting had transitioned painfully to resignation that she would never be a mother. Old women don't get pregnant and bear children, and she had let the dream fade away. Yet she and Zechariah still devoted themselves to serving God and growing in righteousness. Through the pain and social embarrassment, they remained faithful.

Then one day, everything changed. A heavenly messenger appeared to Zechariah and brought the most unexpected news possible!

Introduction

Dawn is twenty-seven and loves Jesus. She has a good job working for a non-profit and finds deep satisfaction in her work. She has three wonderful roommates who get along and seek to encourage one another in their relationships and faith. Dawn has a great life, and she recognizes it. In the midst of this, she has a longing to meet a Christian man who would love her and one day ask her to marry him. This has not yet happened, so she waits and prays. To make things more complex, two of her roommates are engaged and planning weddings. The third is in a serious relationship, and it looks like engagement might be on the horizon. Dawn is happy for her friends, but their joy sometimes becomes a reminder of her waiting.

Emma has been married for eleven years. For the first few years, she and Jesse actually did their part to make sure they did not get pregnant. They wanted a couple of years to build their relationship and create a stable environment for a family. They had worked hard and bought a cute house with two rooms for kids. At the four-year mark, they were in "baby mode" and praying for God to lead this part of their life together. At year seven, after two miscarriages, the waiting had become painful. When they passed the celebration of a decade of marriage, after countless tests and a couple of very expensive procedures, their waiting had led to a sort of numbness of heart.

Jackie works as a computer programmer and has been with the same company for more than a decade. She's a team player and consistently adds value to the projects she works on. In fact, she gets regular affirmation from colleagues and impeccable reviews from her supervisor. What she has *not* gotten is a promotion to be a team leader. She has watched, for more than ten years, numerous other employees move past her into leadership roles that she knows she could do. She has waited, prayed, and wondered why she has not received the thumbs-up to take the next step in her vocational life.

Talk About It

Briefly respond as a group to one of the following questions.

Tell about a time when you waited and waited for something your heart longed for. How did your journey of waiting affect the condition of your heart?

If you have come out on the other side of this waiting season, what is one thing you learned as you waited?

Waiting isn't meant to be passive but to actively stretch us to grow deeper in our relationship with God.

—*Margaret Feinberg*

Video Teaching Notes

As you watch the teaching segment for session eleven, use the following outline to record anything that stands out to you.

Waiting is part of life

God is worth the wait

The story of Elizabeth

God is worth the wait because God is worthy of the wait

Don't miss the One worth waiting for

God is working in the wait

Place the weight of the wait on God

Don't wait alone

You can get so focused on what you're waiting on that you miss the One worth waiting for.

—Margaret Feinberg

Small Group Study and Video Discussion

Take a few minutes with your group members to discuss what you just watched and explore these concepts in Scripture.

1. During the teaching session, Margaret noted that "waiting doesn't have to be a waste, especially when we learn to wait well." What does "waiting well" look like?

   What are ways God can use waiting to grow your faith? What are ways God has redeemed or used waiting to grow you?

2. What are some of the frustrations and struggles that come when we are waiting? If we don't keep the right attitude, where can we go off track, become negative, or even fall into faithlessness during long times of waiting?

3. Often we are tempted to take things into our own hands or question God's plans during times of waiting. In what ways have you done these two things? What are some of the dangers of doing them?

The best measure of how far your focus is off Christ is how hard you're working to stay in control.

—*Margaret Feinberg*

4. **Read** Luke 1:5–7. Tell about a time when you had a dream, a longing, a desire that you prayed and prayed for—but the waiting continued. How did this impact your relationship with God? How did it impact the way you view yourself?

5. **Read** Luke 1:11–17. God's assurance that Zechariah and Elizabeth would have a child came through the visitation of an angel. Describe a time you had a surprising encounter with God, and he gave you hope during a difficult season of waiting.

6. **Read** Luke 1:19–25. Tell about a time you waited, prayed, and maybe struggled, but finally your prayer was answered and joy came. How did you express this joy? How did this moment impact your life?

7. **Read** Isaiah 64:3–5. How can we miss God in the midst of the waiting? How can missing God in the waiting make our waiting even harder?

How does clinging even closer to God during times of waiting redeem these times and make them worthwhile?

8. <u>Read</u> Luke 1:39–45. How can seeing, imagining, or dreaming the bigger things God might be doing through our waiting help us make it through tough times?

Tell about a time that you made it through a significant season of waiting. What were the "bigger things" that God was doing in your life and the world around you?

> *God is worth the wait because he is worthy of the wait.*
>
> *—Margaret Feinberg*

9. Think of several ways you can keep your heart tender and responsive to God during times of waiting. How might you develop one of these practices in your life? How can your group members support and encourage you in this?

10. We need to learn to wait in community. Who is in your "community of waiters"? How do these people support and help you through the hard times of extended waiting?

How can waiting in community fill your soul and help God's work to be accomplished in you? Who do you need to come alongside as he or she goes through a time of waiting?

Most likely, the work that God is doing in your season of waiting is bigger than you. And it's not just about you.

—*Margaret Feinberg*

Closing Prayer

Spend time in your group praying in any of the following directions:

- Thank God that he never leaves you, even in the hardest times of waiting.

- Give thanks to God for the people he has placed in your life who are with you in your times of waiting.

- Pray for eyes to see people who are in a time of waiting and for compassion to care for them and walk with them.

- Confess where you tend to walk through waiting alone. Ask God to give you courage and humility to invite others to be with you in your waiting.

- Admit to God how you tend to take over and try to circumvent the work he might be doing in your life through the process of waiting.

- Declare to God that he is always worth the wait. Commit to hold on to him and trust him, even when the wait is long and things seem dark.

God does not call us to wait alone but rather to wait on him alone.

—*Margaret Feinberg*

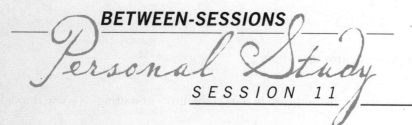

BETWEEN-SESSIONS
Personal Study
SESSION 11

<u>Reflect</u> on the material you have covered during this session by engaging in any or all of the following between-sessions activities. Make a note of any questions or comments that arise from the activities that you would like to discuss at your next group meeting.

Build a "Community of Waiters"

God does not want you to wait alone. Of course, he is always near you through the presence and power of the Holy Spirit. But he also provides people who can be with you during your times of waiting. Today, seek to build a "community of waiters" by actually asking two or three friends to covenant with you to be present in each other's lives during times of waiting. Agree together on what you will do and not do as you walk with each other. The following are some ideas to help you shape your own guidelines:

<u>We will:</u>

- meet together with some regular rhythm;

- pray when we are together;

- pray when we are not together;

- be honest about how we are doing as we are waiting;

- encourage each other to hold to Jesus in the midst of the waiting;

- encourage each other to read Scripture and seek the face of God in our waiting.

We will not:

- give each other easy answers;

- tell anyone else about what someone in our "community of waiting" is going through;

- let our time be a place for negativity and complaining.

Write down the names of the friends you will ask to be in your community, and then record what you agree to do and not do as you wait together.

Possible people to be part of my community:

What we agree to do:

What we agree not to do:

Reconnect

Think about two or three people who have been close friends in the past but you had to separate away from due to a life move or job change. For some reason, in the flow of life these friends have fallen off the radar. Make a commitment to reconnect with these people in some meaningful way. Check in on how they are doing, and be sure to do the following:

- Share what they mean to you.

- Ask for any prayer needs they might have (collect these in the space provided and make a point of praying for them weekly for the coming month).

- Find out how they are doing in this season of their life.

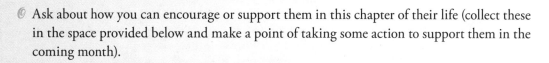 Ask about how you can encourage or support them in this chapter of their life (collect these in the space provided below and make a point of taking some action to support them in the coming month).

Friends I want to reconnect with:

Their needs that I commit to pray for:

Ways I can encourage and support them:

In a month, check in with your friends again. Reaffirm your friendship and assure them you will keep praying for them regularly. Let them know you want to continue growing your relationship, even though you are not in the same location.

Looking Back

One of the best ways to become more accepting of times of waiting is to look back and remember the good things God has done in your heart and life through past seasons of waiting. Use the space provided to chronicle three different times you went through a season of waiting. Reflect on and write down the lessons you learned along the way.

1. What I waited for and how long I waited:

How this season of waiting came to a close (if it has):

Lessons I learned during this time of waiting:

2. What I waited for and how long I waited:

How this season of waiting came to a close (if it has):

Lessons I learned during this time of waiting:

3. What I waited for and how long I waited:

How this season of waiting came to a close (if it has):

Lessons I learned during this time of waiting:

Relinquish control to Christ. Trust in the WHO even if you can't see the WHY or the HOW.

—*Margaret Feinberg*

Journal

Use the space provided below to write some reflections on any of the following topics:

- Write about some of the negative patterns or attitudes that creep into your mind during a time of hard waiting. How can you minimize or avoid these?

- Record some of the positive things you do that honor God and grow your faith in a time of waiting. How can you build on these and develop them?

- Write down some good lessons you have learned and specific ways God has matured you through times of waiting.

- Think about what you are waiting for now. How might this situation be bigger than you realize? What might God do through it that is bigger than you?

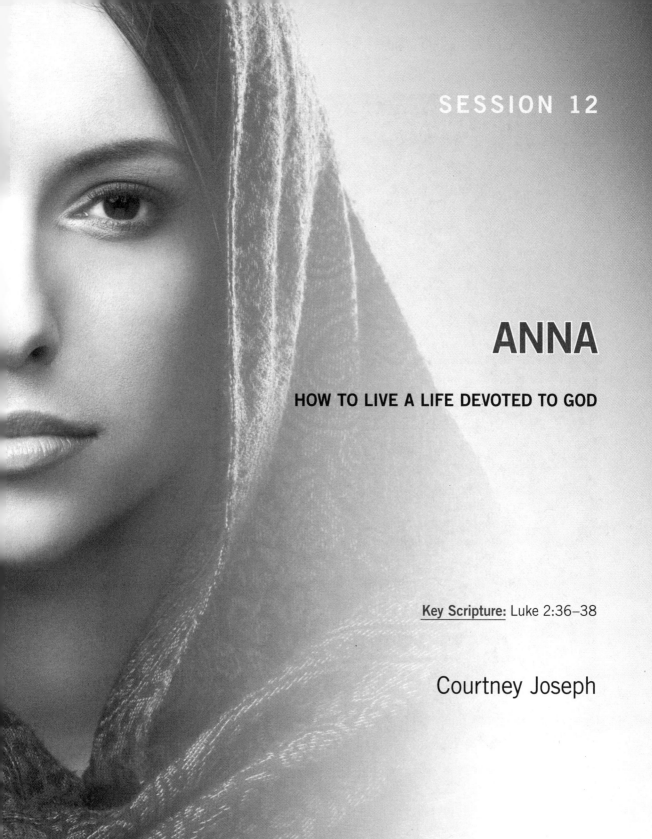

ANNA

HOW TO LIVE A LIFE DEVOTED TO GOD

Key Scripture: Luke 2:36–38

Courtney Joseph

MEETING ANNA

Three short verses in the Bible. That is all we have to open a window into the life and soul of this great woman of faith. Yet in these verses, we encounter a woman whose life speaks to us with a message that is timely and powerful. The truth is, we don't need to know *everything* about a woman to understand her faith. We just need to know the *right things*.

Anna was married for only seven years before her husband died. In her culture, chances were she wed quite young. By the time she was eighty-four (when this story was told), she had lived as a widow for most of her life. That is a lot of years to be alone. Anna was a woman who experienced deep and heart-piercing loss. She also battled all that comes when a person loses a spouse and learns to adjust to a life on one's own.

Anna was Jewish, one of God's chosen people. Her family line could be followed back to Asher, a son of the patriarch Jacob. She was also a *prophet*. Take note of that fact. God spoke to and through this faithful woman. She walked with God, heard from him, and spoke what she learned to others so they could also walk closely with their Maker. As part of her prophetic ministry, as well as the leading of her heart, Anna spent as much time as she could in the temple area in Jerusalem. It was like a home to her.

What is delightful to see in the life of Anna is that she was not simply religious. She did not merely go to the temple and then head home as soon as possible. She lingered there. She marinated her soul in the things of God. She was passionate about her faith and relationship with God. There were three distinct practices of holiness that Anna engaged in as a part of her connection with God: she worshiped, fasted, and prayed. These spiritual disciplines were so much a part of her life that they became who she was.

Indeed, Anna was so saturated in the presence of God that when Jesus was brought to the temple, she recognized him! She saw the redemption of the world wrapped in clothes and held in the arms of Mary. She declared who this was to all who would hear.

In these three brief verses, we learn that Anna was a woman who pressed through loss and pain and held the hand of God regardless of what she faced. She had an intimate relationship with her Maker and ministered in power. Because of this, she was responsive to God's presence and quick to proclaim his truth.

We can discover much from this amazing woman of faith.

Introduction

Ashley seems to always be on the move. Places to go, people to see, and things to do. It is just the way she lives from day to day. When her alarm jolts her awake each morning, she puts her heart, mind, and body in gear and starts going full speed. Some mornings, she has her breakfast on the run because she has commitments that keep her from sitting at the dining room table.

Her day is often a blur of responsibility after responsibility which take her into the evening, with little or no time to slow down. Space for quiet reflection on life seems to be squeezed out most days. The idea of decelerating is not even on the radar. And extended times of prayer and Bible reading feel like a luxury she can't fit into her crazy schedule.

In fact, when she does crack open her Bible or spend a few moments in prayer, it's usually while she is flat on her back, under the covers, and exhausted at the end of the day. She rarely gets past even a few verses before sleep descends on her weary body and mind.

What makes Ashley's frenzied pace so shocking is that she is not a mom of three. She is not seeking to navigate a professional world along with a home life. She is not an empty nester with grandkids and volunteer responsibilities in the community and at church. Ashley is an eighth-grade middle school student who tries to get good grades, plays on two sports teams, seeks to build solid friendships, and really wants to have a strong walk with Jesus.

At her young age, she has already shown signs of stomach problems related to stress. She loves Jesus and longs to slow down, but when? She wonders if maybe high school, college, or some other chapter of adulthood will provide a pace of life that makes room for her to focus on her faith and grow in her love for Jesus.

Talk About It

Briefly respond as a group to one of the following questions.

What kind of advice would you give to a young woman like Ashley who has already let the pace of her life get so ramped up that spending regular quiet time with God seems like a dream she can't experience?

What are some things in your life that cause your heart and mind to race so fast that spending reflective time at the feet of Jesus seems difficult or impossible?

> *Anything less than God himself will leave our souls hungry.*
>
> —*Courtney Joseph*

Video Teaching Notes

As you watch the teaching segment for session twelve, use the following outline to record anything that stands out to you.

A walk on the seashore with two different agendas

God's desire for us to slow down and connect with him

The example of Anna . . . a woman who made daily space to draw near to God

The value of *worship* (showing up) as we await the return of Jesus

The power of *fasting* (the challenges) as we await the return of Jesus

The joy of *prayer* (routines help us) as we await the return of Jesus

The value of reading the words of the *Bible* as we await the return of Jesus

We are all different, but we can all still learn from Anna's example

> *If we don't slow down to be in God's Word and in prayer, we will miss the voice of God in our lives.*
>
> **—Courtney Joseph**

Small Group Study and Video Discussion

Take a few minutes with your group members to discuss what you just watched and explore these concepts in Scripture.

1. Our heavenly Father's desire is for us, his children, to spend time with him. If you are a parent or grandparent, or have a close relationship with a child, tell about the delight you experience when this child or grandchild wants to spend time with you. How do you think God feels about being with you, his beloved child?

2. When you think of God's desire to be with you, what is it that he wants from you as his child? Make a list of three things you believe God wants from you when you spend time in his presence:

   ●

   ●

   ●

Share your list with the group and talk about one of the ways you do a good job of connecting with God and spending time in his presence. Also talk about an area in which you struggle to connect with God but really want to grow deeper.

3. Our Maker wants us to be still and know that he is God. What gets in the way of you being still and fully engaging with God in regular times of quiet and reflection? Conversely, what helps you make space for him?

4. **Read** Luke 2:36–38. What do you learn about Anna's life journey in these verses? What do you learn about her faith? How is Anna's story like that of many women today? How is it unique and an example to us?

5. Anna's faithfulness was rewarded by the joy of getting to see Jesus, the Savior, face-to-face. Describe a season of life when you were faithful to seek Jesus and spent time at his feet as a passionate worshiper. How did this posture of seeking lead to you seeing the face of Jesus with greater clarity and experiencing his presence more fully?

6. Why is regular attendance in worship with God's people so important? What do we gain when we make weekly participation in worship with God's family a priority? What do we miss when we fall out of this rhythm?

7. Fasting is often a forgotten and missed spiritual discipline among Christians today. Why do you think so few followers of Jesus take time to fast (purely for spiritual benefit)? What can help us overcome fear and avoidance of fasting?

If you have fasted as a spiritual discipline and part of your worship of God, tell about your experience. How did you grow? What was challenging? What did you learn about God and yourself?

> *Sometimes the only way to quench our spiritual hunger for God is to fast from physical food.*
>
> —*Courtney Joseph*

8. What other practices, disciplines, or routines have you personally found helpful for staying focused on the Lord?

9. Anna spoke to people as they came to the temple. She told them about Jesus, the One who would bring redemption to the world. How often do you talk to people about your faith in Jesus and your confidence that he really is the Savior of the world? What gets in the way of you sharing your faith freely and confidently?

10. Who is one person in your life who still does not know the love, grace, and redeeming power of Jesus? How can your group members pray for you as you seek opportunities to be bold in talking about Jesus, just as Anna was?

Be devoted to God right where God has placed you.

—*Courtney Joseph*

Closing Prayer

Spend time in your group praying in any of the following directions:

- Thank God for the women in your life who have been an example of passionate faith and following Jesus.
- Ask God for power to resist all the temptations and distractions that can get in the way of you seeking Jesus.
- Pray for a growing desire to connect to God through worship, prayer, and fasting.
- Ask God to give you a renewed and growing passion for the Scriptures and the discipline you need to read the Bible each day with an open heart.
- Invite the Holy Spirit to grow your boldness to tell others about Jesus and all he means to you.

God never forgets his own. He is faithful to his children. He is answering our prayers. We must never stop praying.

—*Courtney Joseph*

FINAL
Personal Study
SESSION 12

<u>Reflect</u> on the material you have covered during this session by engaging in any or all of the following activities. Make a note of any questions or comments that arise from the activities that you would like to discuss with a group member or other friend in the coming days.

Study Fasting in the Bible

The Bible records the stories of many different individuals who engaged in fasting and prayer. Choose three or four of the characters listed below and read their story, paying specific attention to their fasting. Use the space provided on the next page to gather some notes about what you learned.

Character	Passage
Moses	Deuteronomy 9:9–18
David	2 Samuel 12:1–23
Elijah	1 Kings 19:3–8
Ezra	Ezra 10:6–17
Esther	Esther 4:15–17
Darius	Daniel 6:18–23
Daniel	Daniel 10:1–3
Jesus	Matthew 4:1–2
Paul	Acts 9:1–9

What I learn about why they fasted, how they fasted, and what resulted from their fasting:

How this person's life, faith, and fasting could influence my spiritual life:

Review all you learned from these various biblical characters and write down five specific lessons you gathered from their stories.

-
-
-
-
-

In light of what you learned from studying these stories and gathering your own insights on fasting, set a personal goal for fasting over the coming weeks or months.

My goal:

Making a Place to Meet with God

Set up a space to meet with God on a regular basis. Consider using a closet, kitchen table, bathroom, sunroom, special chair, or wherever works for you. It can be simple, or you can really go to town on this project. Remember, the goal is to designate a place to meet with your Friend and Savior, Jesus. Seek to develop a discipline of being in this place at least once a day. You might even want to tell family members or roommates that when you are in this place, you would love it if they would help protect you from distractions so you can really focus on connecting with God.

During your time with God, consider writing out your prayers in a journal if you have not already been doing so. You could buy a nice journal, use an ordinary pad of paper, or even create a file in your computer for this purpose. The type of paper or format is not the real issue—the value of this discipline is to make time to write out your prayers on a regular basis. Try this for a month, adding at least one prayer entry each day.

Rigorously Remove Clutter

During the teaching session, Courtney talked about how the distractions and clutter of busyness can get in the way of us spending quality time with God on a daily basis. So today, consider sitting down with your schedule and doing the following three things:

1. *Remove the things from your schedule that do not directly benefit your life or deepen your faith.* Identify habits, hobbies, TV viewing patterns, online time wasters, and anything that seems to be a recurring and a needless time filler. Guard your calendar. Be vigilant!

2. *Plan to have good quality time with God.* This might sound strange, but actually put God in your schedule. Block out time to be with God daily, at least once a day and, some days, even more. Use the guidelines Courtney talks about in this session that we learn from the life of Anna. Be sure you have time for worship, prayer, study of the Bible, and even fasting. Get this on your schedule, and don't let anything else crowd God out!

3. *Shut down the tech distractions.* Technology can be an amazing gift. It can also be an incessant distraction. So make a commitment to shut down the flow of distracting data while you are making time to be with God. Phones, tablets, and computers actually have an off switch . . . they really do!

Make a commitment to give God your best time, and make sure it is uninterrupted. If you are going to use a device for your Bible reading or journaling, turn off the flow of calls, texts, etc. that will cause your device to ring or vibrate. If you don't know how to do this, get someone to teach you so that you can give God your best time and focus!

*Create routines of worship, Bible reading, prayer, and fasting.
It will sustain you through life's ups and downs.*

—*Courtney Joseph*

Journal

Use the space provided below to write some reflections on any of the following topics:

- Write down the best lessons you have learned about spending time with God from great women of faith you have met.

- Write down the best lessons you have learned about spending time with God from the women of faith in the Bible.

- Record your goals for growing closer to God through worship, fasting, prayer, and reading the Bible.

SMALL GROUP LEADER HELPS

To ensure a successful small group experience, read the following information before beginning.

Group Preparation

Whether your small group has been meeting together for years or is gathering for the first time, be sure to designate a consistent time and place to work through the twelve sessions. Once you establish the when and where of your times together, select a facilitator who will keep discussions on track and an eye on the clock. If you choose to rotate this responsibility, assign the twelve sessions to their respective facilitators up front, so that they can prepare their thoughts and questions prior to the session they are responsible for leading. Follow the same assignment procedure should your group want to serve any snacks/beverages.

A Note to Facilitators

As facilitator, you are responsible for honoring the agreed-upon time frame of each meeting, for prompting helpful discussion among your group, and for keeping the dialogue equitable by drawing out quieter members and helping more talkative participants to remember that others' insights are also valued in your group.

You might find it helpful to preview each session's video teaching segment and then scan the "Small Group Study and Video Discussion" questions that pertain to it, highlighting various questions that you want to be sure to cover during your group's meeting. Before your group meets, ask God to guide the discussion, and then be sensitive to the direction in which he wishes to lead.

Session Format

Each session of the study guide includes the following group components:

- **Introduction**—an entrée to the session's featured Bible woman/theme, which may be read by a volunteer or summarized by the facilitator.

- **Talk About It**—a choice of icebreaker questions that relates to the session topic and invites input from every group member.

- **Video Teaching Notes**—an outline of the session's video teaching for group members to follow along and take notes if they wish.

@ **Small Group Study and Video Discussion**—Bible exploration and questions that rein-force the session content and elicit personal input from every group member; interspersed throughout are featured quotations from the video teacher.

@ **Closing Prayer**—several cues related to the session themes to guide group members in clos-ing prayer.

In addition, in each session you will find a helpful one-page "Meeting . . ." biography on the featured Bible woman, several between-sessions activities for the group members to do during the week, and a guided journal section to allow them to more deeply reflect on the session themes.

Personal Preparation

On a practical level, you will want to bring the following items to each group meeting:

@ Your Bible

@ This study guide and a pen

@ The video and a device on which to play/display it

Enjoy your time together!

ABOUT THE PRESENTERS

Karen Ehman is a Proverbs 31 Ministries speaker, a *New York Times* bestselling author, and a writer for Encouragement For Today, an online devotional that reaches over one million women daily. She has written many books, including *Keep It Shut, Let.It.Go.,* and *Hoodwinked* (with Ruth Schwenk). Married to her college sweetheart, Todd, and the mother of three, she enjoys antique hunting, cheering for the Detroit Tigers, and feeding the many teens who gather around her kitchen island for a taste of Mama Karen's cooking.

Bianca Juárez Olthoff is the chief storyteller for the A21 Campaign and the creative director for Propel Women. She is the author of *Play with Fire: Discovering Fierce Faith, Unquenchable Passion, and a Life-Giving God.* Bianca is a stepmom to Parker and Ryen and has spent the last ten years mobilzing God's people to action alongside her husband, Matt, the executive director and pastor for Project Europe.

Lisa Harper is a gifted communicator whose writing and speaking overflows with colorful pop-cultural references that connect the dots between the Bible and modern life. For six years she was the national women's ministry director at Focus on the Family, followed by six years as the women's ministry director at a large church. She is the author of many books, has a masters of theological studies from Covenant Seminary, and has been a featured speaker with Women of Faith®.

Chrystal Evans Hurst is the coauthor of *Kingdom Woman,* a book that has sold over 100,000 copies. She writes regularly for her own blog, *Chrystal's Chronicles,* as well as blogging for Proverbs 31 Ministries, FortheFamily.org, and TheBetterMom.com. Chrystal is a dedicated wife and mother of five and serves as the chief operating officer of the Hurst household. Chrystal and her husband, Jessie, reside in a small town just outside Dallas, Texas.

Margaret Feinberg is a popular Bible teacher and speaker at churches and leading conferences such as Catalyst and Women of Joy. Her books and studies, including *Wonderstruck* and *Fight Back with Joy*, have sold more than one million copies and received critical acclaim. She lives a beautiful life with her husband, Leif.

Courtney Joseph Courtney Joseph, is a graduate of the Moody Bible Institute with a degree in Evangelism and Discipleship. Her passion and sincerity has made her a leader in the Christian blogging community. She has over 1.5 million views on YouTube and is the founder of the ministry Good Morning Girls, where she is leading women through the Bible, chapter by chapter, cover to cover. She is the creator of the SOAK Bible Study Method and GMG Bible Coloring Chart. Courtney writes at WomenLivingWell.org and GoodMorningGirls.org.

ABOUT THE WRITER

Sherry Harney is an author and speaker for national and international groups. She serves as the leadership development director at Shoreline Community Church in Monterey, California. She is also the cofounder, along with her husband Kevin, of Organic Outreach International, a ministry that trains church and movement leaders to mobilize their members to go into their community and world and naturally share the good news of Jesus.

Over the past twenty-five years, Sherry has cowritten and collaborated on over seventy small group studies with such authors as Ann Voskamp, Christine Caine, Max Lucado, Nabeel Qureshi, Bill Hybels, John Ortberg, Mark Batterson, Gary Thomas, and Dallas Willard. Sherry and Kevin have three adult sons and two daughters-in-law. Sherry loves to hike, ski, read, cook, and hang out with family and friends. She is passionate about living her life with Jesus, like Jesus, and for Jesus.

Twelve Women of the Bible
Study Guide with DVD

Life-Changing Stories for Women Today

Lysa TerKeurst, Elisa Morgan, Amena Brown, Jonalyn Fincher, Jeanne Stevens, Naomi Zacharias with Sherry Harney

In this 12-session video Bible study, some of today's best loved Bible teachers look at the spiritual lessons learned from twelve biblical women and what they mean for your life today.

You'll learn about the triumphs and failures of Mary Magdalene, Rebekah, Hannah, among others, studying their lives and learning how to:

- Apply biblical lessons to your own modern-day struggles
- Live through your failures as well as successes
- Draw near to God in a world filled with trials
- Find lasting contentment
- Overcome rejection and insecurity and much more

The study guide, by Sherry Harney, features background information on each character, video notes, discussion questions, prayer direction, and more.

Sessions include:

1. Eve: Finding Lasting Contentment in the Truth (Lysa TerKeurst)
2. Rebekah: Breaking Free of Feminine Stereotypes (Jonalyn Fincher)
3. Leah: Overcoming Rejection and Insecurity (Naomi Zacharias)
4. Hannah: Surrendering in Waiting (Amena Brown)
5. Abigail: Dealing with Confrontation in Relationships (Elisa Morgan)
6. Gomer: Learning to Accept Unconditional Love (Jeanne Stevens)
7. Mary, Mother of Jesus: Moving from Comfort to Courage (Jeanne Stevens)
8. Mary Magdalene: Transforming from Outcast to Follower (Jonalyn Fincher)
9. Mary of Bethany: Putting Our Faith into Action (Elisa Morgan)
10. Martha: Finding Our Identity in Jesus (Amena Brown)
11. The Woman at the Well: Turning Our Messes into Messages (Lysa TerKuerst)
12. The Syrophoenician Woman: Approaching God with Persistency and Boldness (Naomi Zacharias)

Available in stores and online!

ZONDERVAN®
.com